CHOSEN TO BE A SOLDIER

ORDERS AND REGULATIONS
for
SOLDIERS
of
THE SALVATION ARMY

CHOSEN TO BE A SOLDIER

ORDERS AND REGULATIONS
for
SOLDIERS
of
THE SALVATION ARMY

' Thou therefore endure hardness, as a good soldier of Jesus Christ. No man that warreth entangleth himself with the affairs of this life; that he may please him who hath chosen him to be a soldier '

(2 Timothy 2: 3, 4).

Originally prepared by
THE FOUNDER

Revised and issued by authority of
THE GENERAL

INTERNATIONAL HEADQUARTERS
101 Queen Victoria Street, London EC4P 4EP
1977

Made and printed in Great Britain by
The Campfield Press, St. Albans

GENERAL ORDER

Commanding Officers are responsible for seeing that the soldiers of their corps are acquainted with these regulations and that all intending soldiers are supplied with a copy before or at the time they are given *Articles of War* for signature.   These orders and regulations should be read before enrolment.

TABLE OF CONTENTS

CHAPTER I. SOME FEATURES OF SALVATIONISM

Sect. 1. Nature, Origin and Development of The Salvation Army.

Sect. 2. Articles of War.
Sect. 3. Orders and Regulations for Soldiers.

CHAPTER II. THE NEW BIRTH

Sect. 1. Salvation from Sin.
Sect. 2. The Gift of God.

Sect. 3. God Acts in His Own Way.

CHAPTER III. LIVING WITH GOD

Sect. 1. Life with a Purpose.
Sect. 2. A Life with Practical Value.

Sect. 3. Life Divine, from Jesus Flowing.

CHAPTER IV. MAINTAINING CONTACT WITH THE LIFE GIVER

Sect. 1. The Life of Prayer.
Sect. 2. Studying the Bible.
Sect. 3. Walking in the Light.

Sect. 4. Walking by Faith.
Sect. 5. Witnessing and Working.

CHAPTER V. THE DOCTRINES OF THE SALVATION ARMY

Sect. 1. The Eleven Articles of Faith.
Sect. 2. The Handbook of Doctrine.

Sect. 3. Army Symbols as Expressions of Doctrine.

CHAPTER VI. HOLINESS OF HEART AND LIFE

Sect. 1. The Call to Holiness.
Sect. 2. The Crisis of Sanctification.

Sect. 3. The Holy Life.

CHAPTER VII. RENOUNCING THE WORLD, ITS WAYS AND WORKS

Sect. 1. The World: Mankind in Rebellion against God
Sect. 2. Worldliness

Sect. 3. Worldly Ways and Christian Standards.

CHAPTER VIII. CHRISTIAN STANDARDS OF SEXUAL MORALITY

Sect. 1. How the Army Interprets Biblical Teaching on Sex.
Sect. 2. Courtship.

Sect. 3. Engagement.
Sect. 4. Marriage.
Sect. 5. Unworthy Conduct.

CHAPTER IX. HUMAN RELATIONSHIPS

Sect. 1. With Individuals.
Sect. 2. In the Home.
Sect. 3. At Work.
Sect. 4. With the Neighbours.

Sect. 5. In the Community.
Sect. 6. With Fellow Soldiers.
Sect. 7. With Other Christians.

CHAPTER X. THE SALVATION ARMY, ITS STRUCTURE AND LEADERSHIP

Sect. 1. An Integral Part of the Universal Church.

Sect. 2. As an International Movement.
Sect. 3. The Corps.

CHAPTER XI. THE SALVATION SOLDIER

Sect. 1. A Representative of Salvationism.
Sect. 2. Saved to Save.
Sect. 3. Willing Worker and Glad Giver.
Sect. 4. Public Speaking.
Sect. 5. Lifelong Commitment.

Sect. 6. The Call to Officership.
Sect. 7. The Care of the Body.
Sect. 8. The Improvement of the Mind.
Sect. 9. The Use of Leisure.
Sect. 10. Times of Sickness.

CHAPTER XII. THE ARMY SPIRIT

Sect. 1. A Significant Expression.
Sect. 2. Strong Faith.
Sect. 3. Infectious Joy.
Sect. 4. Burning Compassion.

Sect. 5. Going for Souls and Going for the Worst.
Sect. 6. The Army of the Helping Hand.
Sect. 7. Soldiers Bound for Glory.

ORDERS AND REGULATIONS
FOR
SOLDIERS
OF
THE SALVATION ARMY

CHAPTER I

SOME FEATURES OF SALVATIONISM

SECTION 1. NATURE, ORIGIN AND DEVELOPMENT OF THE SALVATION ARMY

1. The salvation soldier must clearly understand the basic nature of the Movement of which he is a member.

The Salvation Army is a fellowship of people who have accepted Jesus Christ as their personal Saviour and Lord and whose common aim is to induce others to subject themselves to the lordship of Christ.

2. The salvation soldier should know something of the origin and development of the Army he has joined.

In the year 1865 an English Methodist minister, William Booth, at that time 36 years of age, felt the call of God to work for the salvation of the people in the East End of London, where ignorance of the gospel, where drunkenness, crime and vice, as well as poverty, unemployment, overcrowding and other social evils were rife. Working together with volunteers from various denominations, he soon found himself in charge of a rapidly developing movement which eventually was named The Christian Mission. Its structure and discipline became more and more influenced by military usage, and when in 1878 by sudden inspiration William Booth coined the phrase ' The Christian Mission is a

Salvation Army ', this immediately caught the imagination of his nearest co-workers. The former name was dropped, the Movement was officially renamed ' The Salvation Army ', and William Booth, often referred to as ' the Founder ', became its General. There followed the introduction of other ranks, uniforms and symbols, and the gradual adoption of guide lines for organization, discipline and vocabulary ' after the fashion, although not in imitation, of a military force ' as the Founder explained during the 1904 Congress.

This development was wholeheartedly supported by General Booth's gifted and devoted wife, Catherine, whose influence on the life and success of the Movement is fittingly indicated by her name of honour, ' the Army Mother '.

Within two years of its change of name the Movement began to spread beyond the country of its origin, and less than a hundred years later The Salvation Army was active in eighty-two countries.

SECTION 2. ARTICLES OF WAR

1. Though the Army's soldiers (members) are drawn from various cultures, traditions and races, as well as from all levels of society, they have all signed their name to the document called ' Articles of War '. In 1890 it was stated as a regulation that ' every salvation soldier must consider, accept and then sign this document '. This requirement is in force today, as are its reasons, which are reproduced here:

(a) That he may understand beforehand the doctrines, principles and practices to which he will have to conform.

(b) Thinking and praying over these Articles will help him to find out whether he really has the faith and spirit of a salvation soldier or not.

(c) The pledge involved in signing these articles will help him to be faithful to the Army in the future.

(d) They prevent many joining who are not in heart and head with us, and who consequently would be likely afterwards to create dissatisfaction and division.

2. The salvation soldier should reflect upon the significance of the fact that the Articles of War, quoted below, are virtually identical with the original ones drawn up at the end of the nineteenth century. The only major addition is the promise to abstain from the use of tobacco. The Salvation Army shows steadfastness of purpose and refuses to lower its standards or to sacrifice its principles.

3. *Articles of War*

Having received with all my heart the salvation offered to me by the tender mercy of God, I do here and now acknowledge God the Father to be my King; God the Son, Jesus Christ our Lord, to be my Saviour; and God the Holy Spirit to be my Guide, Comforter and Strength; and I will, by His help, love, serve, worship and obey this glorious God through time and in eternity.

Believing that The Salvation Army has been raised up by God, and is sustained and directed by Him, I do here declare that I am thoroughly convinced of the truth of the Army's teaching, that is to say:

We believe that the Scriptures of the Old and New Testaments were given by inspiration of God; and that they only constitute the divine rule of Christian faith and practice.

We believe there is only one God, who is infinitely perfect—the Creator, Preserver and Governor of all things—and who is the only proper object of religious worship.

3

We believe that there are three persons in the Godhead
—the Father, the Son and the Holy Ghost—undivided
in essence and co-equal in power and glory.

We believe that in the person of Jesus Christ the
divine and human natures are united; so that He is
truly and properly God, and truly and properly man.

We believe that our first parents were created in a
state of innocency but, by their disobedience, they lost
their purity and happiness; and that in consequence of
their fall all men have become sinners, totally depraved,
and as such are justly exposed to the wrath of God.

We believe that the Lord Jesus Christ has, by His
suffering and death, made an atonement for the whole
world, so that whosoever will may be saved.

We believe that repentance toward God, faith in our
Lord Jesus Christ, and regeneration by the Holy
Spirit are necessary to salvation.

We believe that we are justified by grace, through
faith in our Lord Jesus Christ; and that he that
believeth hath the witness in himself.

We believe that continuance in a state of salvation
depends upon continued obedient faith in Christ.

We believe that it is the privilege of all believers to be
' wholly sanctified ', and that their ' whole spirit and
soul and body ' may ' be preserved blameless unto the
coming of our Lord Jesus Christ ' (1 Thessalonians 5:
23).

We believe in the immortality of the soul; in the
resurrection of the body; in the general judgment at
the end of the world; in the eternal happiness of the
righteous; and in the endless punishment of the
wicked.

Therefore, I do here and now, and for ever, renounce
the world with all its sinful pleasures, companionships,
treasures and objects, and declare my full determina-

tion boldly to show myself a soldier of Jesus Christ in all places and companies, no matter what I may have to suffer, do or lose by so doing.

I do here and now declare that I will abstain from the use of all intoxicating liquor, from the use of tobacco in any form, and from the non-medical use of all addictive drugs.

I do here and now declare that I will abstain from the use of all low or profane language and from all impurity, including unclean conversation, the reading of any obscene book or paper at any time, in any company, or in any place.

I do here declare that I will not allow myself in any deceit or dishonesty; nor will I practise any fraudulent conduct in my business, my home or in any other relation in which I may stand to my fellow men; but that I will deal truthfully, honourably and kindly with all those who may employ me or whom I may myself employ.

I do here declare that I will never treat any person whose life, comfort or happiness may be placed within my power, in an oppressive, cruel or cowardly manner; but that I will protect such from evil and danger so far as I can, and promote, to the utmost of my ability, his present welfare and eternal salvation.

I do here declare that I will spend all the time, strength, money and influence I can in supporting and carrying on the salvation war, and that I will endeavour to lead my family, friends, neighbours and all others whom I can influence to do the same, believing that the sure and only way to remedy all the evils in the world is by bringing men to submit themselves to the government of the Lord Jesus Christ.

I do here declare that I will always obey the lawful orders of my officers, and that I will carry out to the utmost of my power all the orders and regulations of the Army; and, further, that I will be an example of faithfulness to its principles, advance to the utmost of my ability its operations, and never allow, where I can prevent it, any injury to its interests, or hindrance to its success.

And I do here and now call upon all present to witness that I have entered into this undertaking and sign these Articles of War of my own free will, feeling that the love of Christ, who died to save me, requires from me this devotion of my life to His service for the salvation of the whole world, and therefore do here declare my full determination, by God's help, to be a true soldier of The Salvation Army till I die.

4. Soldiers (including officers of all ranks) are urged from time to time to re-read the solemn undertakings to which they have set their hand and to reaffirm before God their dedication to Him and to His Army, so that their life and service may always be in keeping with the Articles of War.

SECTION 3. ORDERS AND REGULATIONS FOR SOLDIERS

1. The life and warfare of the salvation soldier is dealt with in greater detail in these *Orders and Regulations for Soldiers of The Salvation Army* (1977) which strive to express in an up-to-date way how the Articles of War and the principles these embody must govern Salvationists in an era which has largely abandoned faith in God and Christian ethics.

The salvation soldier of today is thus confronted by new circumstances and may himself at times feel bewildered by the widespread rejection of Christian standards. It is therefore necessary to write with reference to a greatly changed world rather than to endeavour merely to revise the text approved by the Founder for his generation.

2. At the same time the robust faith in God, the spirit of utter devotion to the Saviour and the fervent determination to live to His glory and for the salvation of the people, which were recurrent features of the first *Orders and Regulations for Soldiers*, are just as necessary today for the salvation soldier.

3. This volume, which should be studied by all who contemplate joining the Army and must govern the conduct of all its soldiers, is to be regarded as the authoritative handbook of Salvationism.

CHAPTER II

THE NEW BIRTH

SECTION 1. SALVATION FROM SIN

1. The first and main condition of soldiership is acceptance of Jesus Christ as one's personal Saviour. This is the only way in which any person can pass from the natural state of fallen man into *salvation from sin*.

2. He who surrenders to Christ and accepts the mercy that God offers in His Son, is *converted;* i.e. turned round about from following the path of selfishness, sin and rebellion against God, to walking in obedience to His will.

3. *His sins are forgiven* by God and he stands before his Creator as though he had never committed any evil. He is cleansed from his guilt and possesses a peace which he had not known before.

4. The Bible describes the experience of salvation in many ways, one of which is *being born anew by the Spirit* (John 3: 3-5). This means that the soul is filled with a new life, a life of fellowship with God, and the convert is accepted as the child of God and shares His life.

SECTION 2. THE GIFT OF GOD

1. The *new birth* (also called regeneration) and the *spiritual life*, are two of the mighty works wrought by God in salvation. The convert must not think that he can take any credit for them to himself. What he has done is simply to receive the help without which he would be lost. The whole story of our salvation is a record of God's merciful doing from beginning to end. The Apostle Paul wrote: ' For by grace are ye saved through faith; and that not of yourselves: it is the gift of God: not of works, lest any man should boast ' (Ephesians 2: 8-9).

2. While it is not within the power of any human being to earn, merit or give himself salvation or spiritual life, he can refuse to let God do His work in the soul by not fulfilling the conditions which God demands of him. The sinner must make *confession of his sin to God.* He must admit before God and to himself that his wrong feelings, intentions, thoughts, words and acts are really sinful and therefore stand as a barrier between him and God, until God forgives him. There may also be wrongs that he must *reveal (confess) to other persons;* and if he has caused loss, damage or hurt to them he must be willing to *make restitution* as far as possible. Nor can anyone expect God to save him, if it is his intention to continue in sin. The sinner must have the *sincere intention to give up for ever all that is wrong or doubtful,* to sever harmful connections, and abandon sinful habits. All this marks out the sorrow for sin, the *repentance,* which is necessary if the sinner is to be able to accept Christ as Saviour, the forgiveness of sins which He gives, and the new life which is implanted through the new relationship to the Lord.

3. Another barrier which the sinner can erect between himself and his Saviour concerns *faith.* Saving faith does

8

not mean just that with his mind he accepts the teaching about Christ as true. It means that he is willing to stake his life and his eternal fate upon Christ's promise to receive him, the sinner; to forgive his every sin, and to be his personal Saviour for time and eternity.

SECTION 3. GOD ACTS IN HIS OWN WAY

1. When the soul is born again, the essential proof that the new birth is genuine is not that the process has developed on exactly the same lines as has been the case with some others, or that the conscious experiences conform to those reported by others.

2. Some who have been rescued from a depth of degradation and hopelessness rightly feel that they have gone through a revolution. Others, who have had the blessing of being protected since early childhood from evil of various kinds, have behind them a period of quiet unfolding to the life of faith until the moment comes which resembles the full unfolding of the bud to the splendour of the sunshine. The fact that one's spiritual development fails fully to conform to a set pattern may in fact be an indication that the work of grace, which is directed by the Spirit Himself, has been and is genuinely proceeding.

3. It is enough to accept with heart and will two facts: (*a*) I am not what I ought to be; (*b*) God, who knows what I am, offers me His pardon if I will receive Christ as my own Saviour. He who accepts this divine offer will as truly be born afresh to newness of life as is the ' trophy of grace '. To both, in God's appointed time, will be given the *testimony of the Spirit* attesting with their own spirit that they are children of God (Romans 8: 16), saved from the guilt and dominion of sin and living the new, spiritual life.

4. The fact that God is the one who acts in the salvation

of the soul makes it doubly important for the sinner to pay heed to His insistent call: ' Behold, now is the accepted time; behold, now is the day of salvation ' (2 Corinthians 6: 2).   Weeping over unrepentant Jerusalem, Christ foresaw the disasters that would soon fall upon it because, as He said: ' Thou knewest not the time of thy visitation ' (Luke 19: 44). The urgent need for decision is emphasized in the Army's prayer meetings, usually following the Bible message, when those convicted of sin are invited to kneel at the Penitent-form at once instead of putting off the transaction to which they are called. There is no saving virtue in the Mercy Seat; but the act of kneeling there is a definite response to the divine urge to accept salvation there and then.

CHAPTER III

LIVING WITH GOD

———

SECTION 1. LIFE WITH A PURPOSE

1. Having received salvation and been born again, the soul is called to live a new life, over which God the Father reigns as King, in which God the Son continues His work as Saviour, and in which God the Holy Spirit acts as Guide, Comforter and Strength. Publicly declaring his submission to the Triune God it is fit and meet that the salvation soldier should give as his first solemn promise at his enrolment, by divine help, to ' love, serve, worship and obey this glorious God through time and in eternity '. This then describes briefly and aptly the contents and purpose of the new life in fellowship with God, a life of such quality that it must be described as eternal.

2. The salvation soldier, a member of an Army which strives to be ever active, ceaselessly engaged in holy

10

warfare for its King, must remember that the Lord Himself places as the most important of God's commandments that of loving Him supremely, with every power of heart, soul, mind and strength. The soldier must have his delight not just in God's gifts and help, but in His nature, His holiness, His righteousness, mercy and love.

3. It is a serious mistake to be so preoccupied with living *for* God as not to have time for living *with* God, adoring Him, listening to Him, worshipping Him and consciously resting in His love. We are called upon to ' enjoy Him for ever '. We are to have our minds stayed upon Him. We can glorify God, which is the purpose of our lives, only in the measure in which we allow His glory to fill our souls.

SECTION 2. A LIFE WITH PRACTICAL VALUE

1. The corrective against the danger of indulging in bogus piety instead of living with God and loving Him supremely is given by the Saviour Himself. He couples the first commandment of the Law with the second one which is like it: We are to love our fellow man as we love ourselves. The Bible expresses in several ways that the genuineness of our love for God is tested by our attitude to man. God, who is love, instils into the hearts of those who truly live in harmony with Him, love of a practical kind to their neighbour.

2. The corresponding corrective is expressed in the Articles of War, where love for and worship of God is coupled with service and obedience. We serve God when we further His purposes, and we obey God when we do His will, whether He gives us direct and immediate orders to perform a certain task, or to abstain from a certain course of action, or whether God's standing instructions make plain what He demands from us.

3. The salvation soldier must be aware of the fact that God has ever commanded the Army to serve Him by serving the people both spiritually and temporally. The greatest peril of the human soul is to live without God's salvation. Consequently obedience to God entails willingness to serve Him as His messenger and to do one's part in winning men for Christ. Every soldier is ' saved to save '. But He who came to serve was and is ever concerned about the temporal needs and sufferings of mankind. Therefore every salvation soldier is also ' saved to serve '.

Section 3. Life Divine, from Jesus Flowing

1. Right intention and sincere purpose are pre-requisites of the new life. The truly saved person will wish to show his gratitude to God by endeavouring in all things to please His King and Lord. The salvation soldier will understand that his very position as a soldier constitutes an obligation to walk worthily of his calling. He will not wonder at the exhortation of the apostle to ' work out your own salvation with fear and trembling ' (Philippians 2: 12).

2. This does not mean that man can in any way sustain his spiritual life out of his own resources. The Bible reminds us repeatedly that we are wholly dependent upon God, who alone can give us spiritual life, supplying us day by day with His grace. The Saviour said: ' Abide in Me, and I in you. As the branch cannot bear fruit of itself, except it abide in the vine; no more can ye, except ye abide in Me ' (John 15: 4). He warns His own that if they lose their communion with Him, they will wither and end up as barren branches, in which the life of the Vine no longer is at work.

3. If on the other hand the disciple of Christ maintains his obedience to and faith in the Saviour, the divine life

will fill his being and produce what human endeavours cannot secure—increasing likeness to Christ and deepening love for Him and for his fellows. Our ' fear and trembling ' will concern the fact that we must not allow our connection with the Source of our life to be broken, ' for ', as the apostle continues, ' it is God which worketh in you both to will and to do of His good pleasure ' (Philippians 2: 13).

CHAPTER IV

MAINTAINING CONTACT WITH THE LIFE GIVER

———

SECTION 1. THE LIFE OF PRAYER

1. The salvation soldier must ever bear in mind that prayer is the chief means of keeping in that contact with God in which His life fills the human soul and the Holy Spirit makes the presence of Christ living and real. So wonderful are the possibilities of the life of prayer that those who have penetrated farthest into its secrets are most vividly conscious of the fact that there is much more to learn and far deeper depths to explore.

2. While the child of God may and should turn to his Father whenever he becomes conscious of need, and talk with Him about anything that is on his mind, the way to a life of ceaseless prayer is through the discipline of observing set times for communion with God. It is necessary, before the duties of the dawning day seize his attention, to submit himself to God so that His touch will be fresh upon him. Nor must he conclude the day without reviewing it before Him. And the salvation soldier will wish to lift up his heart to Him at noon, joining comrades all over the world in invocation for the

salvation of the people and for God's blessing upon the Army.

3. Routine is the great enemy of the life of prayer. It must be combated first of all by striving to realize the presence of God. A few moments in silence, the quiet repetition of a suitable verse or chorus, whispering what is known to be true (e.g. ' God is near me. He wants to speak to me. He will help me to listen to Him '), an act of praise and adoration, these and other means will help to this end.

4. It is well, also, to have beforehand a mental or written plan for the season of prayer in which we are about to engage. Points to be remembered should include:

Praise to God for what He is in Himself and to us (e.g. high, holy, beyond understanding; loving Father, mighty Saviour, patient Guide).

Thanksgiving for gifts and mercies to be mentioned by name, both spiritual and temporal.

Intercession for various people; requests for guidance, help, spiritual victory, revival and the salvation of souls (this could be both a general topic and intensely individual).

Accepting God's promise and command for this day.
New dedication.

The Lord's Prayer.

5. It is important not to follow the same plan until it becomes hackneyed or mechanical. Daily communion with God must have the spontaneity and freshness of heart-to-heart talks, in which the one praying is eager to listen as well as to speak. It is useful to settle beforehand how much time is to be spent in communion with God, since there is then greater likelihood of concentrating on this one matter.

6. The salvation soldier must not allow himself to be discouraged by two common difficulties, known even to the greatest saints. His soul is not always filled with delight, as he prepares to engage in prayer. But even a seemingly cold and dry time of worship is often productive of great good. The Holy Spirit prays in and through the sincere, though uninspired soul. A second difficulty is that of wandering thoughts. They must not distress the one at prayer, but should be woven into the pattern of his devotions. Even about them he may speak to his Father.

7. Family prayers should be held wherever a salvation soldier can arrange to do so. Every soldier must recognize the importance of prayer for the life of The Salvation Army and should be ready not only to offer prayer in meetings where such is called for, but to attend all Army gatherings in a prayerful spirit. It is especially important to be present at prayer meetings with faith and expectancy. Soldiers who form prayer circles in each other's homes or decide to observe a regular time of prayer in their own home on behalf of their corps and The Salvation Army are sure to accomplish much more than they can imagine. Many a revival has been given as a reply to the persistent secret praying of a few soldiers; and few exercises are more beneficial to one's own spiritual life than sharing with others the warfare of prayer.

SECTION 2. STUDYING THE BIBLE

1. To the salvation soldier there can be no book as important as the Bible. It is the source from which all Army doctrine is derived. It alone constitutes the divine rule of Christian faith and practice. In order to have a firm grasp of the soundness of what the Army teaches, the soldier must study for himself both the Old and the New Testament. He will find that the Army's doctrinal

position and its standard of Christian living find their warrant in the Bible.

2. The Scriptures are a means of grace. It is the testimony of one generation after another that through them God finds the soul of man and the soul of man finds God. The salvation soldier's spiritual life must be nourished and strengthened, and his walk before God guided and maintained, through the message of the Bible.

3. Bible study is not just a duty of the Christian, which he must fulfil. Reading the Bible as a chore fosters a religious life which is without joy, liberty and power. The salvation soldier should be impelled to read the Scriptures by his love for God, who reveals His gracious will in the Bible, and quite especially by his desire to meet the Lord Jesus Christ, who to the reverent reader steps out from its pages as a living personality, and whose voice is heard through its message. It is the Scriptures that witness of Christ; therefore the soldier finds ever-renewed life in them as well as a living message to proclaim to the world.

SECTION 3. WALKING IN THE LIGHT

1. The Bible calls the life of obedience to the will of God ' walking in the light ' (1 John 1: 7). We are clearly told that we cannot have fellowship with Him unless we do walk in the light. However much we may profess to live the new life, if we disregard the known will of God, ' we lie and do not the truth ' (1 John 1: 6). Even the attempt to come to terms with things about which we are doubtful is bound to disturb our spiritual life. The salvation soldier must be obedient not only to the inward monitor, his conscience, but to that far more sensitive indicator which the Spirit-filled Christian possesses: the peace of Christ which is to rule his heart and mind.

2. Observation suggests that there are three deviations from the road of light which all too frequently are allowed to lead believers away from the walk with Christ. One is a loveless attitude to others. Bitterness, hatred, jealousy and an unforgiving spirit bring darkness to the soul and cause havoc to the spiritual life. Another is the sin of unchastity or impurity—a sin against which the Christian must be unceasingly on his guard in these days of increasing sexual permissiveness. The salvation soldier must walk with Jesus in white, ever trusting in the cleansing Blood. A third is dishonesty, particularly in money matters. The only safe way is one of utter conscientiousness and refusal to entertain even the thought of shady gain. The salvation soldier must ever strive to be like his Master in love for his fellows, in uncompromising purity and absolute honesty.

3. There are two means of grace which are particularly helpful to the Christian who is determined to walk in the light: the ministry of the Bible, and self-examination. ' Not forsaking the assembling of ourselves together, as the manner of some is ' (Hebrews 10: 25), the soul lays itself open to the searching light of God's word, and the faith which helps to overcome the tempter is granted, according to the promise: ' Faith cometh by hearing, and hearing by the word of God ' (Romans 10: 17). Private study of the Bible is not intended to be a substitute for listening to the message in a gathering of God's people. The salvation soldier must neglect neither.

Self-examination is an equally scriptural means of keeping the soul walking in the light. To the Corinthians Paul wrote: ' Examine yourselves to see whether you are holding to your faith. Test yourselves ' (2 Corinthians 13: 5, R.S.V.). The Army's Founder suggested that the soldier should carefully and thoroughly examine the condition of the soul at least once a week. Perhaps the first question that needs to be put is: ' When last did I by faith experience the living presence of the Saviour?' The following questionnaire drawn up by William Booth might also be put to earnest use:

(a) Am I habitually guilty of any known sin? Do I practise or allow myself in any thought, word or deed which I know to be wrong?

(b) Am I so the master of my bodily appetites as to have no condemnation? Do I allow myself in any indulgence that is injurious to my holiness, growth in knowledge, obedience or usefulness?

(c) Are my thoughts and feelings such as I should not be ashamed to hear published before God?

(d) Does the influence of the world cause me to do or say things that are unlike Christ?

(e) Do my tempers cause me to act, or feel, or say things that I see afterward are contrary to that love which I ought to bear always to those about me?

(f) Am I doing all in my power for the salvation of sinners? Do I feel concern about their danger, and pray and work for their salvation as if they were my children?

(g) Am I fulfilling the vows I have made to God in my acts of consecration, or at the Penitent-form?

(h) Is my example in harmony with my profession?

(i) Am I conscious of any pride or haughtiness in my manner or bearing?

(j) Do I conform to the fashions and customs of the world, or do I show that I despise them?

(k) Am I in danger of being carried away with worldly desire to be rich or admired?

SECTION 4. WALKING BY FAITH

1. The new life which is the subject of the present chapter is often referred to as the life of faith. In this

connection faith does not just signify intellectual acceptance of the great truths of Christian doctrine, however important it is to give assent to them. It means, rather, trusting God to be faithful to His promises and to act for the best for His Kingdom and His children.

2. ' Walking by faith and not by sight ' is a biblical expression which stresses the importance of obedient faith in God even when we cannot see or imagine how the path on which we are being led can be right, or even that we are being led at all. The Apostle Paul expresses the assurance of this faith when he says:' We know that all things work together for good to them that love God, to them who are the called according to His purpose ' (Romans 8: 28).

3. Another important reminder is that we are to be led by ' faith, not feelings '. Even the steadiest temperament has periods of ups and downs. Physical, biological, psychological and other factors affect our feelings. The salvation soldier must learn to distinguish between feeling happy and being saved; feeling down and yet, in fact, being upheld by God. Clinging in faith to the promises of God, he will have the same experience as his fellow believers throughout the ages. When they felt weak, they were strong, just because they did not rely on anything of their own.

Section 5. Witnessing and Working

1. The victorious life demands open and courageous confession before other people about one's wish to live as a Christian. At home, at work, in one's daily surroundings one must witness about Christ and His goodness. This does not mean that one presents oneself as a model Christian, but that one makes it clear that one has found the Saviour and wishes nothing more highly than to please Him. Where such witness is given openly yet

humbly and without any intention of casting any reflection on the unsaved, it will often be found that the soldier commands the respect and good wishes of his acquaintances.

2. Glad and sincere witness about Christ generally opens the way to work for Him. Many people welcome the opportunity of a private talk about life's deepest questions. The salvation soldier should see it as his great opportunity to help men and women to find the answers for which they have secretly longed. Such personal evangelism is the special calling and duty of every Salvationist.

3. The question of what friendships to sever and what companionships to maintain will be answered almost of itself, where the salvation soldier is faithful in his witness and work for Christ. The reactions of the people concerned will speak for themselves. It is obvious that companions who wish to make him abandon his faith and his allegiance to Christ are not suitable for the soldier. Many friends will probably disappear when they find that the convert has undergone a change of heart and life. Those who remain will most likely be of the class just described in paragraph 2. So long as the soldier can associate with them as a genuine messenger of Christ, without allowing himself to be influenced by their unconverted nature and interests, he will find that the responsibility he accepts for their salvation will help himself to remain true to the Saviour.

CHAPTER V

THE DOCTRINES OF THE SALVATION ARMY

SECTION 1. THE ELEVEN ARTICLES OF FAITH

1. The Salvation Army has its own confession of faith, which in eleven brief articles expresses the principle doctrines, which the salvation soldier accepts when he signs the Articles of War (see Chapter 1, Section 2). From the beginning such a statement of doctrine was found essential so that people with various—and no— religious background might be united in a common faith, by which they could be governed and which they could all publish. The place of doctrine in the life of the Army is therefore central.

2. The salvation soldier must clearly understand that the Salvation Army Articles of Faith follow the main outline of historic Christian teaching as derived from the Scriptures. The Army Mother stated in 1883 that the Movement was not ' diverse from the churches in the great fundamental doctrines of Christianity ', nor had it ' adopted any of the new gospels of these times '. And the Founder made it clear that the Army had never imagined it would be able to teach anything new in regard to the Christian faith. ' We keep ourselves with all our heart to the three Creeds '. Of these (Apostles', Nicene, Athanasian), the Apostles' Creed and the Nicene Creed appear as Appendices 2 and 3 in the *Handbook of Doctrine*.

3. One function of the Articles of Faith is to safeguard the Army against possible attempts to introduce unauthorized teaching on subjects of little importance to the glory of Christ, the salvation of souls and the sanctification of God's people. The Army will not be party to encouraging divisions in the Church of God by

21

pronouncing on views that must remain speculative and are no part of the universal Christian faith.

4. It is possible to sum up the practical implications of Salvation Army teaching quite briefly.

(*a*) All men are sinners in need of salvation.

(*b*) The atonement made by Jesus avails for all.

(*c*) Conversion is an inward spiritual change wrought by the Holy Spirit.

(*d*) Salvation from sin should lead to holiness of life.

SECTION 2. THE HANDBOOK OF DOCTRINE

1. The salvation soldier has at his disposal a carefully prepared, theologically competent and easy-to-follow help to the study of the Army's teaching, called the *Handbook of Doctrine*. This should be one of the first Army publications which he should master. It will help him to be rooted and grounded in our holy faith and to give a reason for the hope that is in him. The book will amply reward repeated study.

2. The teaching contained in the *Handbook of Doctrine* will also help the soldier to maintain the spirit of Christian love for all God's children, whatever their race, culture or confession, who with him accept the two great Creeds of the universal Church.

3. The *Handbook of Doctrine* will make it clear to the salvation soldier why the Army's eleven Articles of Faith contain two or three statements which appear to speak of obvious matters. They are warnings against some deadly errors. Thus Article 6 does not just express the clear scriptural truth in which we glory that 'whosoever will may be saved', but protests against the terrible doctrine that God has predestined some souls to be eternally lost. Articles 7 and 9 seek to correct the mistaken notion held

in some quarters that faith which is *not* joined to repentance or obedience is, nevertheless, enough to obtain salvation.

4. In an appendix there is explanation why the eleven Articles contain no reference to the sacraments and why The Salvation Army does not administer them. It emphasizes that the Army does not on that account sever itself from other sections of the Church or condemn their use of the sacraments.

5. The *Handbook of Doctrine* gives a careful exposition of the tenth Article of Faith, which refers to the Army's convictions on the subject of a holy heart and life. The same subject is treated in the next chapter of these regulations, but because of its great importance the salvation soldier should carefully study the teaching of the Handbook as well as reading the Army's holiness literature in general.

SECTION 3. ARMY SYMBOLS AS EXPRESSIONS OF
DOCTRINE

1. A symbol is ' a sign which produces a uniform social reaction '. The significance of a symbol is not clear from the sound, thing, happening, etc. which constitutes it. Its significance is made clear only through teaching and mutual agreement between those who use it in their communication.

2. The Army's motto '_Blood and Fire ' is a symbol. It was taken into use in order to reduce Salvation Army doctrine into two powerful words; words that refer to the most significant in the second and third articles of the Nicene Creed: ' I believe . . .

   (*a*) ' in one Lord Jesus Christ . . . who for us men and for our salvation came down from heaven ',
   (*b*) ' in the Holy Ghost, the Lord and Giver of life '.

3. The Salvation Army salute is a symbol. It consists in raising the right hand above the shoulder with the first finger pointing upward. It is a token of recognition and salvation greeting used by Salvationists of all ranks in every part of the world. The salute is a reminder of their common homeland, heaven, and of their aim to win others for the Kingdom of Heaven. The salute is suitably accompanied by a joyous ' hallelujah! '

4. The flag is a combination of four symbols, each with its own significance:

(*a*) The motto ' Blood and Fire ', explained in paragraph 2.

(*b*) The main colour, which is red, stands for the Blood of Jesus Christ.

(*c*) The yellow signifies the Fire of the Holy Spirit.

(*d*) The blue is a reminder of purity of the soul which is washed in the Blood and baptized by the Fire.

Not only does the flag thus bring a reminder of the central truths in the Army's message, but it is emblematic of the aggressiveness of salvation warfare and is a reminder of God's dealings with the Army in the past. It is also a symbol of the internationalism of the Army and a constant call to faithfulness and renewed dedication to God and the Army.

5. The crest is also a combination of symbols, no fewer than seven, and represents the leading doctrines of the Army:

(*a*) The round figure—the sun—represents the light and fire of the Holy Spirit.

(*b*) The cross in the centre represents the Cross of our Lord Jesus Christ.

(*c*) The letter ' S ' stands for salvation.

(*d*) The swords represent the warfare of salvation.

(*e*) The shots represent the truths of the gospel.

(*f*) The crown represents the crown of glory which God will give to all His soldiers who are faithful to the end.

(*g*) The motto ' Blood and Fire '—see paragraph 2 of this section.

Symbolizing as it does the leading doctrines of the Army, the crest as a whole may therefore be regarded as the symbol of The Salvation Army.

CHAPTER VI

HOLINESS OF HEART AND LIFE

———

SECTION 1. THE CALL TO HOLINESS

1. Right from its beginning The Salvation Army has been convinced that God's plan of salvation does not only aim at the forgiveness of sin, the justification of the sinner, great and glorious though this basic work of God's mercy is. The Army believes that Jesus Christ Himself established a standard for His followers—in the words of Catherine Booth—' a standard not only to be aimed at, but to be attained to—a standard of victory over sin, the world, the flesh and the devil, real, living, reigning, triumphing Christianity '. The Army is therefore both a revival and a holiness Movement.

2. The spiritual change known as conversion is the commencement of sanctification, of the work of being separated from all that is displeasing to God, and of being dedicated to His use and developing a Christian character. The Bible states emphatically and in many ways that ' for this purpose the Son of God was manifested, that He might destroy the works of the devil ' (1 John 3: 8). The saved person must see it as a strong call to allow Christ's purpose to be fulfilled in his life, so

25

that he is freed from self and sin, cleansed from defilement, and transformed to live in holy love.

3. The salvation soldier who knows the Lord Jesus and lives in fellowship with Him feels the call to holiness as an obligation. Moreover the perfect revelation of holiness which Christ's life and character display must surely fill the Salvationist with an intense longing to be like Him. Christlikeness is in fact the best description of holiness. There is something seriously wrong with the spiritual life of any Christian who does not earnestly strive to become wholly devoted and obedient to God, strong and upright, true, pure, kind, loving and humble, —in one word, holy like Jesus.

SECTION 2. THE CRISIS OF SANCTIFICATION

1. The salvation soldier, whatever his personal experience, must beware of declaring that a holy life which displays true Christlikeness is impossible. All too often such a declaration betrays an indifference to the whole subject of holiness which is in itself a serious indictment. It is tantamount to claiming that one had done everything humanly possible in order to conquer temptation and sin, even resisting unto blood, and yet without victory. It could be, however, that behind such a statement there are sincere endeavours to live as an overcomer, but even repeated failures do not warrant the sweeping conclusion. The likely explanation is that the secret of the holy life has not yet been grasped. Instead of dropping the subject, let the soldier ' follow after holiness '. The promise is that those who seek shall find. This happens in the crisis of sanctification.

2. It may be that the crisis primarily consists in judgment on ' an evil heart of unbelief '. The soul, tired of its failures, must nevertheless be reminded of the obvious truth which the *Handbook of Doctrine* (Chapter

26

10, Section IV, 1(*b*) and (*c*)) states thus: ' Man cannot be holy unless he is delivered from sin . . . There is one means of deliverance—that provided by the Atonement. The announcement of the gospel is that God wills and has made it possible for men to be set free from sin. The Risen Saviour is the supreme antagonist and conqueror of sin (see Romans 6: 1-11).'

3. The divided heart is often the real maker of mischief in the spiritual life. The Danish philosopher Søren Kierkegaard used to say: ' Purity of heart is to will one thing.' In the crisis of sanctification the seeking soul sees and acknowledges that the heart is not ' perfect before the Lord ', but wants to retain some things for its own use. Consecration to God is not complete. Mixed motives are revealed. God's will is not fully accepted. Secret reservations are brought to light; in the crisis God is implored to rid the soul of these and to unify the divided will. And He does it. He grants the seeker a clean heart.

4. The despairing heart, weary after a long period of trying to live without condemnation yet ever experiencing shortcomings and failures, despite its sincere resolves, its renewed endeavours, and its many attempts in faith to accept the blessing of holiness, makes the great discovery in the crisis of sanctification. God who has worked in him to *will*, is also able to work in him to *do* His good pleasure. The emphasis shifts from man's own endeavours to the mighty working of God. The Holy Spirit reveals to the seeker the secret of holiness, which Paul expresses for his own part by saying: ' I live; yet not I, but Christ liveth in me: and the life which I now live in the flesh I live by the faith of the Son of God, who loved me and gave Himself for me ' (Galatians 2: 20). With that discovery, the pursuit of holiness changes from a demand to a privilege. The Spirit makes the presence and

fellowship of Jesus living, real and most precious to the sanctified soul.

5. The salvation soldier should realize that the holy life is the secret of the spiritual power of the Army as well as of his own soul. He must not rest content with anything less for his own part. He will do well to study what the *Handbook of Doctrine*, Chapter 10, has to say on the subject of sanctification. The Army also has a treasury of books and articles on the same theme and in addition the doctrine of holiness is expounded in holiness meetings. But the soldier must understand that no descriptions of the experience of sanctification can be more than helps to holiness. He must entreat the Holy Spirit to be his Teacher. Only the Spirit knows the special needs and problems of the individual soul, and only He can apply to man's mind and heart the truth that sets him free.

SECTION 3. THE HOLY LIFE

1. At times the crisis of sanctification has been understood as an experience by virtue of which the soul will be living the life of holiness. This is true only in the sense in which it can be said that a successful operation makes it possible for a patient to enjoy full health. If he does not take care of his health he will soon be far from well, despite the fact that the operation was a success. Holiness is a divine work. It is God who sanctifies, and it is He who keeps the heart and life holy. All holiness has its source in the holiness of God. There is no such thing as holiness apart from ' Christ in you '.

2. Above everything else the holy life is therefore a life of constant fellowship with the Saviour. It is true that the believer's safety is associated with Calvary and that he must look upon the Sinbearer who suffered there *for*

him. The ever-confirmed assurance of the forgiveness of sins is an unfailing defence against the devil. But the believer is also to identify himself with Christ *on* the Cross, as being crucified *with* Him and fully united with Him and He with the believer, so that the Saviour's death means the death of his old nature, leading to a new life in the power of the Resurrection. The holy life is thus a life possessed by God's transforming grace and therefore separated from a life of sin and failure. By faith and obedience the sanctified soul keeps himself in the love of Christ.

3. The holy life is not a life of such maturity and perfection that no further development or progress is possible. It is a life where the heart is pure, that is to say, where the will is undivided and kept steady by the love of Christ for the believing soul and by the soul's consequent love for Christ. But the Holy Spirit, by whom the love of God is poured out in the soul, so that the believer becomes overwhelmingly conscious of the wonder of being the object of the divine love, ever instructs the sanctified soul concerning the way in which this mutual love is to govern the whole life both in regard to the relationship to God and to fellow humans. Here new insights are always possible, and the character can grow ever more Christlike.

4. Holiness of heart and life is thus marked by the grace of love, the spiritual gift to be sought above all others, *the* fruit of the Holy Spirit. It is marked by the glad acceptance of the greatest commandment of all, the commandment to be loving, even towards people whose attitudes could provoke to unconcern, bitterness, self-assertion, enmity, strife and the like. In such circumstances the love of Christ helps the sanctified Christian to show concern, helpfulness and forbearance for others. The salvation soldier will pray to be kept so

29

near to God that he is truly a testimony to the power of Christ to sanctify and endue the soul with holiness, or ' perfect love '.

CHAPTER VII

RENOUNCING THE WORLD, ITS WAYS AND WORKS

SECTION 1. THE WORLD: MANKIND IN REBELLION AGAINST GOD

1. At times the word ' world ' is used to denote the whole of mankind and indeed God's entire creation, without wishing to indicate any opposition of the creature against its Creator. In this sense it can be said that God loves the world. But the Bible also urges believers not to love the world nor to be conformed to its ways, but by faith to overcome it, keeping themselves unspotted by the world. ' The world ', used in this way, means the opposite from the Kingdom of God. It stands for humanity refusing to be subject to God, to acknowledge His sovereignty and to obey His commands.

2. Rebellion against God has been the curse of mankind throughout the ages. It gives free rein to the spirit of selfishness, self-aggrandizement, lust for power, disregard for others, cruelty and falsehood, which is characteristic of unregenerate human nature. This is the spirit of the world; of the realm whose prince is Satan.

3. The world today provides terrible examples of the consequences of rebellion against God. It is said that faith in Christ is not necessary for the maintenance of ethical standards and that mankind has come of age and does not need the prop of religious faith. ' At last the human spirit is free ', it is claimed, with the abolition of

moral standards once thought self-evident, and consequent uncertainty, hopelessness and anguish. Lawless-
ness and terror abound, with disregard for human life.
In this situation those who do not have a firm conviction
about the view of life through Christian eyes may experience a deep sense of insecurity.

SECTION 2. WORLDLINESS

1. The salvation soldier must be careful to distinguish
between the spirit of the world, which is worldliness
properly so called, and its manifestations. Rebellion
against God can be demonstrated openly, coarsely and
contemptuously, or in the guise of refined ' neutrality ',
cultivated ' tolerance ', religion without God, Christianity
without Christ, and many other ways. A worldling is a
person who is taken up with himself and applies a false
scale of values, unrelated to the will of God.

2. The soldier fights for the Kingdom of God. It is
obvious that he must not allow in himself the spirit of
the world. Nor will he have anything to do with what he
sees to be a manifestation of that spirit. Yet he will not
make the mistake of condemning as worldly such things
as dressing neatly or keeping himself well groomed,
appreciating beauty, culture and wit. But he must
beware lest he lives in the spirit of self-absorption, where
these things, commendable in themselves, may testify
that he is worldly-minded. Especially is the desire to
follow the very latest fashion likely to come from such
motives. At times deliberate dowdiness and disregard of
beauty may be an inverted sign of the same spirit of
worldliness. Contempt of others, coupled with self-
satisfaction, is worldliness in essence.

3. Renouncing the world's sinful pleasures, companionships, treasures and objects is a matter to be taken very
seriously. There are amusements which cannot but sully

the soul, e.g. some films and plays. Modern dances are
at times deliberate means of inflaming sexual feelings, a
pursuit which, divorced from pure and honourable love,
is not in harmony with Christ's standards. Companionships must be watched. If it is obvious that old friends
are trying to use their influence to lead the soldier back
to the world, there is no other safe course than to terminate such associations. ' Treasures and objects ' could
be, for example, infidel literature and pornographic
pictures; but anything, from money to so-called status
symbols of any kind, used to make a person look more
important than others who have not the same resources,
is certainly a sign of vanity and worldliness.

Section 3. Worldly Ways and Christian Standards

1. After the declaration of uncompromising and final
renunciation of worldliness the Articles of War mention
some particular points on which the Army's convictions
are strongly against what is practised by many worldly
people and even some Christians. If in some respect
any would-be soldier should query the Army's strict
attitude, he must decide nevertheless faithfully to abide
by it, or else to abandon every thought of joining the
Army.

2. The salvation soldier must abstain from the use of
all *intoxicating liquor* (alcohol), from the use of *tobacco*
in any form, and from the non-medical use of all *addictive
drugs*. Recourse to stimulants, such as *alcohol*, which
suspend the exercise of the highest faculties of the mind,
may lead the unsuspecting first-timer on toward the road
to ruin. As a Movement dedicated to the rescue of
alcoholics, we know the ease with which the old craving
for alcohol can be rekindled. That is one reason for the
total abstinence expected of every salvation soldier. His

example must support and encourage those who know that for them there can be no half-measures. Social drinking to please the host or hostess at some celebration, or the temptation to make alcohol available to a business associate, is ruled out by the pledge given by every member of what has been called the largest total abstinence organization in the world, The Salvation Army. The attitude to the *non-medical use of addictive drugs* is equally uncompromising. The havoc wrought by the use of narcotics has been steeply increasing in recent years. Some argue that soft drugs such as cannabis products are harmless. Medical research does not uphold this and, further, many who experiment with these progress to the use of hard drugs such as opium (and its derivatives, morphine and heroin), cocaine, LSD and methedrine, becoming addicted to them with consequent mental and physical deterioration. Pushers aid this progression with diabolical cunning. Addictive drugs may be prescribed therapeutically and doctors have to supervise such use most carefully. This includes barbiturates and other soporifics. The use of *tobacco* in any form was discouraged in the first edition of the soldiers' regulations on the ground that it was:

　(*a*) injurious to health;

　(*b*) unclean;

　(*c*) a waste of money;

　(*d*) a disagreeable infliction upon others;

　(*e*) an unnatural habit of self-indulgence.

Soldiers who used tobacco could hold no office in the corps. Medical evidence and public opinion have since then given strong support to these arguments. In 1975 it was decided that no person who uses tobacco in any form can in future be accepted as a soldier. The Articles of War were amended to take in a corresponding declaration of abstention.

33

3. *Gambling*. Gambling has developed into a social evil with which the soldier will have nothing to do, in whatever form it appears, whether it be betting on horse-racing, etc., sweepstakes, lotteries, raffles, football pools, bingo and other forms of gambling. Gambling operates on the un-Christian basis of belief in luck and for this reason above all the Salvationist will not gamble. The appeal to the gambling instinct can get such a hold on people that they are led into neglect of their duty to feed and clothe their families, or that they make themselves guilty of dishonesty in order to pay for the stakes etc. At some places of employment some such arrangements are promoted in order to raise money for a charitable purpose. The salvation soldier will make an outright contribution in cash for the same purpose rather than take part in gambling.

4. *Debt*. Debt is a great evil. It destroys a man's peace, makes him feel like a slave, and has a bad effect upon his example.

If debt is such an evil, then it must be a salvation soldier's duty to keep free from it. On no account should he contract debt unless he can see in the most confident manner his ability to meet it when the claim falls due.

Anyone in debt at the time of his conversion must resolve to pay his creditors at the earliest opportunity and should immediately tell them he will do this.

Where a soldier is seriously in debt, the Divisional Commander is authorized to make careful inquiry into the circumstances of the case. Should it be found that a soldier is in a position to discharge the liability wholly or in part, and is not making a reasonable effort to do so, his name may be removed from the roll.

Modern business methods include various arrange-ments involving sales on credit, with ordered repayment over an agreed period of time (instalments system, hire purchase, credit cards, mortgages, etc.). Before entering upon such contracts, the Salvationist will carefully consider whether he may reasonably expect to be able to meet the obligations involved. He must leave a margin for running expenses and for unexpected demands. Prospective married couples should beware of accepting liabilities based on two wages.

Salvationists will resist the temptation to live above their resources.

5. Two distressing symptoms of the moral deterioration of our generation are the increasing use of *vulgar and profane speech* and the deliberate cult of *obscenity and pornography*. These testify to a coarseness and crudity of character which are of grave consequence to the individual and the community. The salvation soldier must beware of the subtle influence of the world in these respects. He must not allow his reactions against vulgarity and swearing in general (particularly in literature and the mass media) to be blunted. He will abstain from vulgarity and obscenity himself and will not hesitate to protest against it. Salvationists pledge their adherence to Christian standards in their dress, deportment and conversation. They condemn the obtrusion of obscenity on the public in the form of suggestive theatre placards and pictures and the exhibition of pornographic literature in public places. They fight to keep themselves unsullied ' from all impurity, including unclean conversation and the reading of any obscene book or paper ' as well as from viewing pornographic pictures, films and exhibitions of any kind. The same standards will determine what television and radio programmes the soldier will allow in the seclusion of his home.

6. Knowing that the Lord desires truth in the inward parts, the salvation soldier pledges himself to practise absolute *honesty*, both in matters of great import as well

as in trivialities of daily life. There is no guarantee
that the honest person will always benefit from his
honesty. The secretary who refuses to type a dishonest
letter may suffer loss of employment; and the one who
uses the firm's postage stamps for personal letters may
not be discovered. But even though the salvation soldier
should have to suffer for the sake of honesty, he must
never resort to falsehood, dishonesty or untruthfulness.
The idea that falsehood which does not hurt a private
person but a group, e.g. the State or a corporation, is
permissible, is totally unworthy of a Christian. Pilfering
from a place of employment or a department store is
also wrong.

Salvationists must by example and precept contribute
to the strengthening of a public opinion which condemns
falsehood in statements issued by any authority, and the
colouring of facts in the mass media and in political
propaganda. Christians have a right and duty to crave
reliable advertising and verity in the words of one individual to another. The promise to deal truthfully,
honourably and kindly with the other party, whether one
is employer or employee, includes the paying of a fair
wage and the rendering of an honest day's work.
Especially must young people with income expect to
carry a fair share of the family household expenses. In
contrast to the worldly principle Paul says: ' Let no one
seek his own good, but the good of his neighbour '
(1 Corinthians 10: 24, R.S.V.).

7. To have responsibility for and *authority over another
person* is a test of character. The worldly spirit takes
advantage of such a position, and this spirit is seen
on a large scale in our time and generation. The Christian
standard forbids the use of a fellow-being as an instrument. Every man, woman and child has human rights.
The salvation soldier must ever remember that the Lord

regards our treatment of others as our treatment of Him. The more helpless and dependent, the more our neighbour should be the object of our care and kindness. The salvation soldier is specially called to stand up for those who are being oppressed because they are ' different '. We must show love for the weak and wayward. And we must never be guilty of inflicting the cruelty of humiliating any person before others. Should we notice someone suffering that mortification, it is our duty to come to the rescue, restoring courage and confidence. This certainly applies to children, who may receive lifelong damage through heartless treatment, but who will bless for the rest of their lives those who recognize them as persons. If we show a person, young or old, such respect and love, we shall be better able to offer that help which salvation soldiers must always supply. The chief human need is to experience love. The Salvationist must strive to satisfy that yearning, God helping him.

8. When the Salvationist boldly shows himself ' a soldier of Jesus Christ in all places and companies ' he achieves several important things:

(*a*) He will not find it difficult to recognize and to avoid the various expressions of worldliness which otherwise might become a spiritual danger to him.

(*b*) He will understand that certain things which would be lawful and harmless to him could cause bewilderment to the newly converted who have experienced the emptiness and hurtfulness of the sinful ways and works of the world. As a soldier of Christ he will gladly abstain from such things for the sake of his new brothers and sisters in Christ.

(*c*) His life as a soldier of Jesus Christ will bring conviction of sin and a call to repentance to some, while others may react by showing him hatred. As a consequence he may have to endure jibes and even persecution. For this he will be prepared. But he will experience the blessedness that the Master has promised His followers in such circumstances (Matthew 5: 10, 11).

CHAPTER VIII

CHRISTIAN STANDARDS OF SEXUAL MORALITY

SECTION 1. HOW THE ARMY INTERPRETS BIBLICAL TEACHING ON SEX

1. The story of creation in Genesis concludes with the arrival not only of Adam but of Eve. The relationship between the sexes is a theme running throughout the Bible creating much of its drama—demonstrating the finest and foulest in human nature. Christ recognized sexuality as God's provision for the enrichment of mankind. It of course ensures the continuation of the race, but beyond this, as the most profound and enduring of human relationships, some of the sublimest experiences of life arise from it. This basic urge is constantly exploited for commercial gain; many films, novels, advertisements deliberately aiming to create sexual stimulation, more likely to arouse lust than lasting affection. But in the creative tension of marriage ever deeper and more selfless affection is fostered. A truly balanced outlook on life requires this psychological sharing between men and women. In the enduring sexual relationship of marriage the home is created and the Bible shows this setting of family life and primary human relationships to be the purpose of God. It follows then that the Salvationist will have a responsible and disciplined attitude to sex.

2. The New Testament letters reveal a society in which sexual immorality was rife. Into this sordid, selfish and

perverted interpretation of one of the most powerful instincts of mankind, the gospel of Jesus Christ came as a cleansing, liberating force. It established a morality in which both motive and act are related to an ultimate standard, a realm of lasting values rather than immediate, physical gratification. There is little doubt that the world still needs the witness and example of Christian living, but the salvation soldier may well be considered narrow-minded and even killjoy by those who have never truly understood Christian standards. The Salvation Army accepts a natural and biblical interpretation of sex. This emphasizes a unity between physical and spiritual dimensions in human personality. It also lays specific stress on sexual relationships as interpersonal ones requiring responsibility for another. It removes thought and deed from the area of guilt and disgust which so many men and women sadly experience. Convinced that the sex act belongs exclusively to marriage, the Salvationist cannot accept the concept of unfettered sexual experimentation.

No one can become or remain a soldier of The Salvation Army unless this is understood and sincerely accepted.

Section 2. Courtship

1. The Salvationist needs to learn to mix happily in Christian worship and service and in social and recreational activity with members of the opposite sex.

As such a friendship deepens the Salvationist will be wise to take thought. The choice of a life-partner is one of the most serious decisions of a life-time, perhaps the most serious. It is the choice of a destiny, of happiness or misery, the heaven of deepening love or the hell of constant friction.

2. *A Salvationist will choose a Christian believer for a marriage partner.* This is in keeping with the scriptural

39

injunction, ' Be ye not unequally yoked together with unbelievers: for what fellowship hath righteousness with unrighteousness? and what communion hath light with darkness? ' (2 Corinthians 6: 14). The sharing of religious convictions is very important in the intimacy of home-life. Disagreement at this level makes unlikely any prospect of a truly happy marriage. If two people are already ' one in Christ ' there is every hope that their marriage will be the sacrament that God intends. The ideal situation, of course, is when both partners are Salvationists.

The Salvationist needs a kindred spirit as a partner. Quite apart from religious affinity there needs to be a wide area of general agreement in other matters. Tastes and ideas need not be identical, but a common approach and similar interests help to give stability to a relationship. Sharing is the essence of marriage.

The momentous decision concerning a life-partner will not be without recourse to prayer. It should be possible to think of the prospective partner and of Jesus Christ at the same time. Some of the happiest marriages in the Army have been contracted between young people who prayed for their coming partners before they knew who he or she was to be.

Should the Salvationist be considering the question of officership, the folly of commencing a relationship that will adversely affect this important issue must be recognized.

Having considered these factors and made a decision, how then will the Salvationist behave? It is obviously wrong for either sex to make advances or to encourage approaches without any serious intention. All relationships must be honest and straightforward.

The young Salvationist will take his parents into his confidence and ask for their advice. His Commanding

Officer is also available for this purpose, as well as other officers.

There should be a clear recognition on both sides that courtship is a test of personal compatibility. Court-ship should be treated seriously, but there is nothing final about it. Most authorities in these matters are in favour of long courtships followed by brief engagements.

Time must be given to allow the relationship to grow, but during this period the Salvationist's service in the Army should not be allowed to suffer.

The Salvationist will not allow impulse or passion to obscure his judgment or encourage unworthy conduct.

In the joy of each other's company, the realization that kissing and caressing are really the preliminaries to the full expression of sexual love will necessitate self-restraint. Each must hold the person of the other in the highest regard.

Consideration for the other person must always be the determining factor. A man or a woman does not always know what the other can endure in the way of close physical contact without pressure becoming too much. An increasing sensitivity to the reaction of the other is needed. To act selfishly is the denial of true love.

SECTION 3. ENGAGEMENT

1. The courtship that develops normally leads naturally to an engagement, which involves a promise to marry. Engaged couples are committed to each other to such a degree that in some countries the breaking of an engage-ment can lead to legal action. Jesus said that in all our commitments our ' Yes ' must mean ' Yes ' (Matthew 5: 37), and that is certainly true in so serious a matter as engagement.

Before entering into an engagement, the Salvationist will consider all aspects of the situation. What prospects are there for marriage? Unless there is a firm hope of marriage in the near future entry into engagement should not be considered.

In Jesus' day, the Jews regarded ' betrothal '—the equivalent to our engagement—as binding as marriage. From Matthew 1 : 19 we know that Joseph could not have put Mary away without a bill of divorcement. Our modern engagement is not as binding as that, but the seriousness with which it is regarded, even by secular authorities, underlines its full significance. A broken engagement is preferable to a miserable marriage, but it is wrong to enter into this obligation until mutual love can make the promise of loyalty with complete conviction.

2. Three matters that should be discussed between the engaged persons are:

(a) *Health*. A medical check-up for both parties is advisable. There are impediments to sexual intercourse and hereditary traits which may or may not be a bar to marriage. However, only a doctor can give sound advice on such matters. Should either party feel that advice given at such an interview is unconvincing or unintelligible it is always possible to obtain a second opinion.

(b) *Money*. The setting up of a home needs discussing, with complete understanding and firm agreement on all financial matters within marriage.

(c) *Children*. Questions relating to the hoped-for family will raise the issue of birth control. Each needs to know where the other stands in this matter. The Salvation Army leaves the question of contraception to the conscience of the individual Salvationist, but expects an attitude of informed responsibility.

3. The Salvationist will not allow himself to be

influenced by those films, plays, magazines and books which suggest that experimentation is advisable and that the full expression of sex is legitimate for engaged couples.

The Christian standard has always been, and still is, that the full expression of sexual love needs to be kept for the marriage union itself.

No act can ever be undone, and this is true concerning sexual union. The two people concerned can never return to what they were before. Both are changed. This is why both bride and groom have the right to know whether or not the other has had prior sexual experience.

The physical expressions of love during the engagement period must be given serious consideration by each couple. It should not be a case of ' How far is it right to go?' Engaged couples are bound to desire to possess and to be possessed, but they need to feel comfortable in each other's company. Lest tensions become too great, excessive petting must be avoided.

Even during the engagement, marriage is still uncertain. In this world there is always the possibility that something can happen to break the relationship.

The argument that a child may result from pre-marital sexual relationships is usually countered by the assertion that this need not happen. In fact, no contraceptive is infallible or fool-proof. No Christian man will subject a woman to the risk of conceiving a child outside of marriage.

In some countries the right to terminate an unwanted pregnancy (abortion) is granted by law. The danger here is that the sense of the sacredness of life may easily be lost. There may be circumstances where abortion can be regarded as permissible, but these must be the exceptions. Abortion should be allowed only on adequate medical grounds, both physical and psychological, such as in the case of rape, or if the health of the mother is at risk. It is not to be sanctioned simply for social reasons. Abortion is not automatically justified in cases of moral laxity and irresponsibility.

The sex act needs the context of marriage and home for its full appreciation and expression. Marriage should possess a sense of newness and this cannot be if sexual union has been already experienced.

SECTION 4. MARRIAGE

1. Christian marriage is the life-long union of one man and one woman, who have promised each other faithfulness. Sexual fidelity is the absolute standard. Marriage is in principle indissoluble. Every salvation soldier must reject the godless mental reservation that if marriage is not a success, divorce is always possible.

Falling in love just happens, but married happiness is something two people create. A good marriage is an achievement.

Marriage is the sharing of life *at all levels*, and this is the ideal to be borne in mind throughout the periods of friendship, courtship and engagement. The Salvationist will be properly concerned about the quality of sharing that is possible and likely in the marriage relationship.

Salvation Army principles concerning marriage are set forth in the following Articles of Marriage to which all officers and soldiers who marry under the flag give their consent:

(*a*) We do solemnly declare that we have not sought this marriage for the sake of our own happiness and interests only, although we believe these will be furthered thereby.

(*b*) We promise that we will not allow our marriage in any way to lessen our devotion to God and our service in The Salvation Army.

to all concerned should be motivated by Christian love.

The question of the continuing soldiership of divorced persons will inevitably arise. Each instance needs to be judged on its merit, as does the question of remarriage of divorced persons within the Army.

SECTION 5. UNWORTHY CONDUCT

1. Sexual misconduct is an offence against the law of love, since it is a gratification of selfish desires without Christian respect for the personality of the other party. This is true even where the partner is equally eager to follow such a course. The sexual urge is not in itself tantamount to love, and where it is allowed to determine action without love and respect, it is more properly called lust.

If a soldier or recruit fails to live up to the Salvationist standard of sexual morality, such failure cannot be ignored by his leaders. These are charged with the responsibility of taking action as required by the appropriate Orders and Regulations (*Orders and Regulations for Senior Census Boards*, Section 5, paragraphs 9–11).

2. No person can become or remain a soldier who is co-habiting with a person of the opposite sex to whom he/she is not married. Persons living together must either marry or separate. This rule cannot be waived for financial reasons, as when taxation laws in certain countries make the taxes on a married couple heavier than on unmarried persons with the same joint income living together, or when a widow loses her pension on re-marriage.

3. In cases of marital infidelity, deliberate promiscuity, a criminal sexual offence or any misconduct of a sexually deviant kind, which can be proved beyond reasonable doubt, there can be no alternative to the removal of the name(s) of the offender(s).

4. The term ' misconduct of a sexually deviant kind ' includes homosexual acts (if between women, termed lesbian practices). It is necessary here to distinguish between homosexual tendencies and homosexual practices. All that has been written in this chapter refers to heterosexual relationships, i.e. between men and women. The homosexual person is attracted to persons of the same sex. This psychological deviance, so long as it does not express itself in homosexual acts, is not blameworthy nor should it be allowed to create guilt. Such persons need understanding and help, not condemnation. Some can never achieve a heterosexual relationship, but it must be remembered that some men and women who have actually committed homosexual acts are still capable of heterosexual relationships. It is well for him or her to engage in types of service other than as leaders of children and adolescents of his/her own sex, so as not to be overwhelmed by the affection which arises between leaders and led. Given a close walk with the Saviour and the strict discipline of thought and obedience which all Christian life requires, there is no reason why the homosexually disposed believer should not be a victorious Salvationist.

Homosexual practices unrenounced render a person unacceptable as a Salvation Army soldier, just as acts of immorality between heterosexual persons do.

5. Those soldiers who do not marry for whatever reason will learn to sublimate their sexual energy, i.e. to divert its creative drive and deep affection into other pursuits. The Salvation Army owes an immeasurable debt particularly to those who have served Christ with undivided energy.

CHAPTER IX

HUMAN RELATIONSHIPS

————

SECTION 1. WITH INDIVIDUALS

1. The Salvation Army soldier cannot escape finding human relationships difficult at times. Little good is achieved by passing harsh judgment on others, whether silently in one's own mind, behind their backs in conversation with others, or even to their faces. If the soldier is to help them he must not first of all settle in his mind how different they ought to be, but how he himself ought to act. Has he developed the kind of personality, social skills and emotional stability which will enable him to react to other people as a Christian, and so to help them?

2. People we may find difficult are often unhappy people. They may seem to us to be deliberately nasty. But their past history is imperfectly known to us. It may be that they have never experienced true kindness and love. Perhaps they had to suffer humiliation and harshness or deliberate injustice in a critical period of development. Whatever the reason, kindness and love coupled with firmness are likely to work a cure.

3. In order to help a person in distress of whatever kind, the would-be helper must be genuinely interested in him or her. He must encourage his charge rather than merely correct and criticize. If we look for faults—we shall find them in plenty. But if we look for good points, we shall certainly find some. If we expect something better, we shall perhaps create an appetite for progress.

4. It is not only difficult people who are likely to benefit by contact with those who care. The suspicious

49

and shy ones are also helped by people who can win them by being ' wary as serpents, innocent as doves '. And salvation soldiers should, in all their dealings with others apply the words of the Master: ' All things whatsoever ye would that men should do to you, do ye even so to them: for this is the law and the prophets ' (Matthew 7: 12). It will be easier to have satisfactory relationships if we do not forget the advice of the Apostle Paul: ' If it be possible, as much as lieth in you, live peaceably with all men ' (Romans 12: 18), and keep in mind the exhortation in verse 10 in the same chapter: ' In honour preferring one another '.

5. All salvation soldiers should strive after that relationship with the Great Physician which makes their health of soul and heart stand up to the test of everyday dealings with their human surroundings. Only thus can the soldier be an evangelist among the individuals whom he meets.

SECTION 2. IN THE HOME

1. Confessing Christ is nowhere more essential and nowhere a greater responsibility than at home. Conversion being life's most revolutionary event, it is right and proper to make known to those with whom a person shares daily life that he has seen his need of God's forgiveness and has accepted Christ as Saviour. Such a confession should be accompanied by a humble request for forgiveness for whatever has been wrong in his life at home and by an expression of his sincere wish to live a Christian life there. Especially if accompanied by a request for understanding and help, this first testimony is likely to make a personal impression on at least some members of the family, provided there is no suggestion of arrogance in it.

2. The effect on others could, however, be a negative one. For reasons of their own they may find it distasteful, they may object to it or scoff at it, and the convert may have to endure persecution. He should bear it with patience and in no circumstances retaliate. Provided that he lives a consistent life, the opposition will probably be short-lived and may lead to the salvation of the scoffers. If endured for Christ's sake this trial will prove a blessing to his own soul, and if by kindness and courtesy he heaps live coals on the head of an opponent he gives the most effective witness possible to the glory of Christ (Romans 12: 20).

3. The relationship between husband and wife, if both are saved, must be marked by the fact that they love the same Master and are fellow Christians. Each is responsible for the other's soul, and when the misunderstandings and frictions arise which are difficult wholly to avoid even in the happiest marriage, they should not let sunset find them still nursing their anger (Ephesians 4: 26). Readiness to ask for and grant forgiveness must mark the relationships with each other of those who love the same generous Lord. Praying together and interceding for each other will help to keep the relationship sweet. So will little acts of love and pleasant surprises. Both husband and wife should be ready to bear each other's burdens, without insisting on what is the work of the man or of the wife.

4. The salvation soldier who is joined to a non-believer will of course pray without ceasing for the conversion of the partner, and will be specially careful by thoughtful love and unselfishness to ' adorn the doctrine of God our Saviour ' (Titus 2: 10).

5. The relationships between parents and children begin to take shape before the birth of the child, when daily prayer will be offered for the expected little one.

The promises made before God in the act of dedication are bound to influence the parents' relationships to their child. The child is dedicated to God in a Salvation Army ceremony, and the parents promise to be examples of true Salvationists seeking to lead the child to love Him and do His will and endeavouring to train the child to be a faithful soldier. It is the privilege and the duty of Salvationist parents to give their child the experience of safety and love, which is a necessity, from his first days of existence, if he is to develop into a harmonious human being. The child's first teaching about God and His love will be the responsibility of the parents. They will introduce the little one to the Saviour and though they will beware of making him precocious, they will share the conviction of the Army that a child can have a conscious meeting with the Saviour at an early age. The holding of daily family worship in the home is of great value.

6. It is important to train children to follow Christian standards of behaviour. They must be taught the difference between right and wrong. Firmness and consistency is necessary, and deliberate wrong-doing must not be overlooked. Punishment must not be arbitrary, but rather must arise as a logical consequence of the wrong to be corrected. Anything in the nature of injustice must be carefully avoided. Children and young people will welcome a certain discipline; but injustice can only work havoc.

7. Salvation soldiers will wish early to introduce their children to The Salvation Army and will expect them as a matter of course to attend the activities for young people at their corps until they have reached the age of discretion. By that time they will, it is hoped, have made a personal decision for Christ and will volunteer to remain or become junior or senior soldiers. Nothing in the nature of compulsion or coercion must be exercised.

Salvationist parents may find their teenagers difficult to understand and handle. Parents should seek to be well-informed regarding this period of human development, when young people are no longer children yet not adult, and still in need of the discreet help of their elders.

8. In their mutual relationships, Salvationist children will need to recognize their responsibility for each other and should be trained to pray for each other. Teenagers must understand that growing up does not excuse rude behaviour, lack of self-control or of respect for parents and others, including those in positions of authority. A tender conscience and a living contact with the Saviour are happily possible in the years of adolescence.

9. The future of the children is of necessity an important question to the parents also. It will always be the service of God which has priority and the parent will endeavour to guide the child in discovering and in doing His will. It may be done in any walk of life, but the Salvationist will always regard officership as a high calling for his children. With this in view the children should be given the best education possible.

SECTION 3. AT WORK

1. To the salvation soldier the first consideration in regard to employment should not be money, holidays, free time, the likelihood of promotion, etc., for in all honourable walks of life Christians are servants of Christ and must therefore make the question of His will and His interests their foremost concern. This was the principle applied by the first edition of the *Orders and Regulations for Soldiers*, speaking about opportunities to better one's position. The soldier's conduct, it was stated, ' must ever be influenced by the consideration as to whether such changes will increase or decrease his

opportunities for saving souls and extending the Kingdom of God '.

2. In whatever relationship the soldier finds himself to those at his place of employment—whether he is their workmate, employer or employee—his life must be such that he can command their respect and trust. He will be willing to help his fellow workers and to defend their interests. He must be a just employer, who does not try to take advantage of their dependence upon him, but treats them courteously and generously. He must loyally and faithfully render the best service of which he is capable in return for the salary or wage he is receiving. While these various positions may not of themselves create opportunities for personal evangelism at a place of work, his Christian life and conduct will invite his fellow workers to talk freely with him.

3. The soldier may have to endure chaffing or even hurtful treatment, but he will not retaliate nor regard himself as a martyr. Sooner or later he will find an opportunity of doing his persecutor a good turn or showing him some kindness, which will make him change his attitude. The soldier will not be slow in seizing the opportunity of influencing him for Christ.

4. Not all work has the same positive value. The Salvation Army has always discouraged its soldiery from working in breweries or distilleries, for this would not harmonize with our total abstinence ruling. The tobacco and gambling industries must be regarded in the same way. The Salvation Army has the duty to urge a basic consistency between its principles and the daily work of Salvationists.

5. Compared with the ' servants ' referred to in the New Testament the situation of workers today is vastly

different, but the advice given is valid (see Ephesians 6: 6–8). Christians will not be content to do as little as possible, only working when under scrutiny; they will do their work as service to Christ.

Trade unions have become a permanent part of the economic scene, their basic function still being to represent the interests of the members.

For managers, the welfare of the workers will usually be one consideration among many. It is therefore necessary and proper that there should be an organization to represent the workers, lest misunderstandings occur and exploitation be allowed.

6. It is in order for the Salvationist to join a trade union and to become active in its affairs. Trade unionism may well be one of the areas in which it is possible for him to make a Christian contribution. The Salvationist will not support decisions which are opposed to the common good and which are dictated by individual, group or political selfishness.

Differences sometimes occur between employees and employers where mutual agreement is not reached. The use of the strike weapon then comes under consideration. A strike is a trial of strength and resolution between labour and management. In all democracies the right for workers to withdraw their labour is recognized.

It is impossible to give advice covering every eventuality but, generally speaking, a worker is likely to be able to accept the democratic decision of his union. There may be occasions when this is not so, and in that case the Salvationist will follow the dictates of his conscience; similarly, he will always refuse to victimize others who, for conscientious reasons, are unable to agree with the verdict of the majority of their fellow members.

7. In every instance the Salvationist, guided by the teaching of Jesus, is expected to bring to his decision an informed mind and a sensitive conscience.

The Salvationist employer will seek to take his employees into his confidence; he will consult with them on all relevant matters. The worker needs to feel he has some influence in his daily occupation. This means that wise management realizes the proper place trade unions have in every industrial situation.

The Salvationist employer will recognize that economic activity involves human beings. There may sometimes be a conflict between what is efficient and what is right. Because economic life is part of God's creation, the demands of love and justice must take first place. Human beings must not be sacrificed to the profit motive. The Salvationist employer will recognize a wise stewardship over the human and material assets entrusted to him. In a capitalist society the latter will be the money of many investors, in a socialist state the property of the nation, and the Salvationist responsible for such, whether on the shop floor, or in an executive office will respect this trust.

> Forth in Thy name, O Lord, I go
>   My daily labour to pursue,
> Thee, only Thee, resolved to know
>   In all I think, or speak, or do.
>
> Thee may I set at my right hand,
>   Whose eyes my inmost purpose see;
> And labour on at Thy command,
>   And offer all my works to Thee.
>
> *Charles Wesley.*

SECTION 4. WITH THE NEIGHBOURS

1. The reformer Martin Luther, commenting on the fourth supplication in the Lord's prayer, remarked that

when asking God to give us our daily bread, we include petitions for other necessities of our daily life. One of these was to his mind ' faithful neighbours '. Those who lived nearest to a family were in those days specially important to the family's own life.

2. In many parts of the world with giant cities and huge blocks of flats, the position nowadays is largely otherwise and people live for years hardly knowing their next-door neighbour. In such circumstances the Salvationist must be frank and helpful. Neighbours should refrain from behaviour that causes annoyance to each other. If differences arise, the Salvationist will attempt to resolve such with patience and courtesy. He will pray for his neighbours and give help in any manner possible. This is particularly the case in times of sickness and bereavement.

3. Unkindness and persecution on the part of neighbours may no longer be a common occurrence, but should a soldier have to bear such, he should do so patiently and without resentment, and if there is injury, he must not resort to retaliation. He will not be overcome by evil, but will overcome evil with good.

4. A soldier should live on friendly terms with his neighbours. He will endeavour to introduce the all-important subject of salvation, not forgetting to give a word of testimony and inviting them to meetings when an opportunity presents itself.

5. Should there be quarrels, ill-feeling and gossip between neighbours, the soldier should endeavour to be a peace-maker and to bring about good relationships between all.

SECTION 5. IN THE COMMUNITY

1. Though a salvation soldier should regard himself as

a pilgrim and a stranger in this world, and though his chief concern must be the Kingdom of God, he is also a citizen of his own country and a member of the community in which he lives. As such he has some influence on its affairs through the exercise of the franchise. It is important that the local and state Government should be in the hands of persons of integrity and ability. Salvationists should therefore give sufficient interest to public affairs to be able to decide which candidates for public offices are most likely to act according to Christian principles and therefore most worthy of their votes.

2. Salvation soldiers must remember that the Army does not identify itself with party programmes in politics and will not therefore endeavour to influence the voters within or without its ranks, except so far as party declarations reveal an inimical attitude to freedom of conscience, moral issues, religious faith and the proclamation to young and old of the gospel of Christ.

3. Should a soldier be invited to stand for office in local or state Government, he should weigh the issues carefully keeping his Salvation Army service as a paramount responsibility. He may wisely discuss the matter with his Army leaders at corps, divisional or territorial level.

4. Many good causes and many essential modes of community service are likely to awaken the sympathy of the salvation soldier. He should remember, however, that his voluntary work for the benefit of the community should be undertaken mainly through the medium of The Salvation Army, which holds a unique position of confidence and rarely has as much man-power as its opportunities demand. The soldier should resist the temptation to be associated with other undertakings for the sake of

personal prestige. He should remember that above all other duties, that of being a personal evangelist will determine how he employs his time and his strength.

5. As a member of an international Movement the Salvationist will not be a narrow nationalist. Because he belongs to God, he is primarily a citizen of the world.

The Salvationist will regard war as an evil, and condemn the use of force as a means of settling differences between nations. The individual has the serious, personal responsibility of deciding on what basis and under what circumstances he could support the use of arms.

Paul urged the Christians of his day to ' submit to the supreme authorities ' and to discharge their obligations: ' Render therefore to all their dues: tribute to whom tribute; custom to whom custom; fear to whom fear; honour to whom honour ' (Romans 13: 1, 7). But occasions have arisen when civil disobedience has been the right Christian response.

To take civil and social responsibilities seriously will always be the Salvationist's attitude, but in the ultimate it is God who must be obeyed (Acts 5: 29). The Salvationist is concerned with service to his fellow-men, the rooting out of injustice and inhumanity and the securing of good government. He desires to see a truthful press, an honest police force, good welfare facilities and just laws.

6. The Christian faith declares that God is the Creator of all and that His providence is world-wide. The differences between races and cultures have introduced suspicion, fear and hostility between groups. It is these that are evil, not the differences themselves. God's action in Jesus Christ was for the purpose of re-uniting mankind. Paul wrote: ' There is neither Jew nor Greek, there is neither bond nor free, there is neither male nor female: for ye are all one in Christ Jesus ' (Galatians 3: 28).

The Christian Church, whenever it is true to its ministry of reconciliation, overcomes the alienation between races. It is a community of faith enjoying and expressing a unity that transcends racial differences. Unfortunately, it has not always lived up to this ideal. From its inception The Salvation Army's witness that the gospel is for the ' whosoever ' was a recognition that God ' hath made of one blood all nations of men for to dwell on all the face of the earth ' (Acts 17: 26). Men should live together as one family. The sacrifice of Jesus on the Cross was God's central act in unifying mankind under His own rule. Every Salvationist will therefore work for racial harmony, knowing this to be the will of God. He will deprecate, and seek to eliminate, unjust discrimination of every kind. He will begin by dealing with any prejudice that may exist within himself.

SECTION 6. WITH FELLOW SOLDIERS

1. Talking about the obligation on salvation soldiers to work for the salvation of the people, William Booth strongly emphasized that the essence of true religion is the love of God shed abroad in the human heart, which prompts a man to serve God and his fellows. ' If the flame of love burns low, the soul will be weak,' he stated. ' If it dies out, the soul ceases to live.'

2. The New Testament makes it clear, however, that the Christian must quite specially love his fellow believers. Those who work for a common Master, knit together by love to those for whom their Saviour died, must of necessity love one another. Paul spoke of the need for having ' the same love, being of one accord, of one mind '. He proceeded ' Let nothing be done through strife or vainglory; but in lowliness of mind let each esteem other better than themselves ' (Philippians 2: 2, 3).

3. Such a loving relationship between fellow soldiers is not ruled out by differences of taste and temperament, or varying opinions and habits. But it does mean sincere appreciation of each other's worth and the heartfelt wish to be of blessing, help and encouragement to each other. Kindness, courtesy and practical assistance is given gladly and without stint. Fellow soldiers whose relationship is one of Christian love will pray for each other, thank God for each other and speak well of each other. The love of Christ makes them sensitive to the need of special encouragement caused by times of trial and difficulty, and tactful help will be quickly forthcoming.

4. The experienced soldier will keep a watchful eye on those who have been recently sworn-in. As recruits they were probably the subject of much kindly interest. They must not be made to feel that no one remembers them once they have become full members of the corps. It is not fair to expect that they will be conversant with all the traditions and practices of the Army. At times they may feel uncertain and forlorn. The loving soldier will reassure them and endeavour to make such newcomers feel at home in the corps life, where they need to know that they are fully accepted.

5. Another class of comrades who should be the recipient of kindly attention are those who for various reasons seem to have lost or be losing their first enthusiasm and spiritual zeal. Such comrades could become backsliders and they may need to be shown much Christian love and kindness.

6. Finally there will be young people who are not yet stable in the faith and who may be sensitive or resentful of discipline. Experienced comrades with a concern for the future generation of Salvationists can be of untold help by showing them loving-kindness, patience and appreciation.

7. Should the life of the corps be threatened through internal differences, every effort must be made to restore peace and effect a reconciliation. It is up to all concerned to show humility and Christian love, and not to insist on their own rights or opinions. They should meet together and, after prayer, talk the matter over, each being willing to concede something to the other. It may be well to do so in the presence of the Commanding Officer, or some other Salvationist in whom the parties concerned have confidence. If this does not bring about a satisfactory conclusion an approach may be made by the comrades concerned through their Commanding Officer to the Divisional Commander. In no circumstances may salvation soldiers go to law with respect to any differences between them. Local officers and soldiers have the right, if no less cumbersome procedure can solve the difficulty, to use the official inquiry procedure, provided by *Orders and Regulations governing Commissions of Inquiry.*

SECTION 7. WITH OTHER CHRISTIANS

1. The salvation soldier sees and accepts whole-heartedly the logic of the saying that the closer Christians live to Christ, the closer they will come to each other. He will regard as brothers and sisters in Christ all those who confess Jesus as Lord and Saviour and will wish to show them kindness and Christian love.

2. The soldier will fully understand that other Christians feel specially attached to their own church or denomination; he will not take offence if some do not seem fully to understand or approve of the Army's position within the universal Church because of certain doctrines and practices. He will not be impressed by the claim of some believers that their particular community is the only one which possesses the whole truth and can

claim subjection to its authority by all who wish to be saved. Nor will he ever claim for the Army that it is perfect in every respect.

3. On the other hand the salvation soldier will rejoice in the Army's firm stand for those biblical teachings which are common to the universal Church and which alone are necessary and sufficient for salvation. He will not therefore experience any need to apologize for the Army's concentration on the message that Christ is able ' to save them to the uttermost that come unto God by Him ' (Hebrews 7: 25), but will steadfastly reject peculiar and sectarian doctrines which some would present as essential. He will pray that God may use the work of other Christians, and he will devote himself to the soul-saving warfare of his own Army.

4. The salvation soldier will not argue with other Christians on differences of doctrine or service. Let them worship their Saviour together and then, each in his place, do the work he has been given to do.

CHAPTER X

THE SALVATION ARMY, ITS STRUCTURE AND LEADERSHIP

SECTION 1. AN INTEGRAL PART OF THE UNIVERSAL CHURCH

1. Unlike many Christian bodies, The Salvation Army has right from the beginning felt it necessary to emphasize the unity of the Church of Christ and to avoid anything that might encourage further division within Christianity.

Instead of proclaiming itself as a church it has throughout its history stressed its wish to remain ' an integral part of that universal fellowship of Christian believers known as the Church of which Christ is the Head ' (*Orders and Regulations for Officers of The Salvation Army*, Introduction, page v).

2. It has thus been the wish of The Salvation Army not to oppose other Christian bodies, but to promote the Kingdom of God. William Booth expressed this by saying that Salvationists do not see it as their God-given task to *protest* against the doctrines or practices of other Christians, but to *attest* the gospel message about the saving work of Christ.

3. The salvation soldier must therefore never interfere with the Christian work done by other bodies, but rather treat them with respect and pray that God may use them to bring sinners to Himself. He must not belittle their doctrines and practices or get involved in arguments about them. At the same time he must ever remember that God's main purpose for the Army is the winning of sinners who are away from God and out of touch with the churches.

4. For practical purposes The Salvation Army has increasingly come to be the church of its own people and of large sections of the people. It is therefore felt right and proper that the Army should take part in the endeavours to promote unity, understanding and practical co-operation between the various Christian bodies.

5. Though The Salvation Army thus sees itself as an integral part of the Universal Church, it remains wholly autonomous and is not bound by any decree or decision of others.

SECTION 2. AS AN INTERNATIONAL MOVEMENT

1. Though at work in an increasing number of countries and nations, The Salvation Army remains one and undivided, an international force under a unified supreme command—The Salvation Army *in* the various countries, not *of* the various countries. All Salvationists have the responsibility and privilege of participating intelligently and sacrificially in the missionary outreach of the Army. The centre of the Army's world-wide administration is International Headquarters in London, England.

2. The Movement's world leader is the General for the time being. He or she is elected by the High Council, consisting of all Commissioners on active service and of all other Territorial Commanders who have held the full rank of Colonel for two years or more. The General appoints his Chief of the Staff, who acts as the Army's Second-in-Command, and also the International Secretaries. Each of these is entrusted at International Headquarters with the oversight of the work in a segment of the world. Other departments at International Headquarters serve the whole Army world in specialized work, such as world finance, Army literature and music, etc.

3. The internationalism of The Salvation Army is of utmost importance both as a spiritual principle and a practical form of organization. It demonstrates the truth that in Christ there are no such dividing forces between believers as national prejudices, class consciousness, sex divisions and other hindrances to full Christian fellowship as sons and daughters of God. It also makes it possible for help to be directed where it is most urgently needed in the form of manpower and means. This principle has stood the test of two world wars, so that the Movement has emerged unscathed and intact as soon as communications were again possible between the various parts of the

Army world. The possibility of disruption from national differences is diminished by the fact of the General's supreme authority. Thus a common international policy is preserved. Though the General as world leader holds the supreme authority, he cannot depart from the accepted and agreed main lines of the Movement. Corresponding limitations of the authority delegated by the General to leaders in lower positions make the Army's system of leadership both safe and flexible.

4. The leadership within a territory is delegated by the General to the Territorial Commander appointed by him. A memorandum of appointment defines in greater detail how the provisions of the *Orders and Regulations for Territorial Commanders and Chief Secretaries* are to be applied in the territory. On many matters the Territorial Commander must hear the recommendation of special boards and report them, as he submits his own opinion to International Headquarters for decision.

SECTION 3. THE CORPS

1. The corps is the basic unit of the evangelistic purpose of the Army. On its work and wellbeing depend the usefulness of the Army in the territory. Its main task is to lead people to a saving knowledge of Jesus Christ. The work is under the leadership of the Commanding Officer, who will delegate some duties to his Assistant Officer or, if a married man, to his wife.

2. The salvation soldier does not hesitate to repeat the words of Paul: ' I am not ashamed of the gospel of Christ: for it is the power of God unto salvation to everyone that believeth . . . for therein is the righteousness of God revealed from faith to faith ' (Romans 1: 16, 17). Wherever people are induced to listen to the preaching of the gospel, its saving power is still as manifest as ever.

3. *The Senior Corps:*

(*a*) In addition to public meetings which aim at the presentation of the gospel to the unsaved, and which are generally called salvation meetings, there are gatherings concerned with the teaching of the doctrine of sanctification and therefore named holiness meetings; soldiers' meetings for the education and training of Salvationists; meetings held by such branches of the work as the home league, which is an association of women designed to inculcate Christian standards in personal and home life; demonstrations and musical festivals, etc. It will be seen, therefore, that the holding of meetings indoors is an important form of the corps work.

(*b*) Very important also is the holding of evangelical meetings in the open air. This must be regarded as a vital outreach and be capable of local variation using door-to-door visitation, personal contact with bystanders, etc. Therefore each soldier must strive to be present and participate.

(*c*) Since the gospel is preached first and foremost in meetings, one of the most important tasks of the corps is to induce people to attend the meetings. By being himself present, by doing his best to persuade others to attend and by witnessing to the truth of the gospel in personal testimony each soldier can take part in this the most essential work of his corps and of the whole Salvation Army. Sensitive to the Holy Spirit, the soldier will be ready to offer prayer both in the meeting itself and in the ensuing prayer meeting, when volunteers are invited to pray.

(*d*) The soldier will pray for each meeting and make intelligent preparation to take part himself. All soldiers must understand and be prepared to play their part in the prayer battle after the salvation meeting, when the unsaved are pressed to make a decision for Christ. Where the Holy Spirit has been working through the meeting, hearers will have been led to conviction of sin and of the necessity to accept salvation. To take this step is not always easy, and therefore the soldier will endeavour to encourage such a person by talking with him and exhorting him to rise and go forward to the Penitent-form. Such a conversation with a soul under conviction is often called 'fishing', an allusion to the Saviour's promise that His followers would become fishers of men. At the Penitent-form the soldier will kneel with the seeking person, pray with him, help him to confess to God, guiding him until he is willing in obedient faith to accept Jesus Christ as his Saviour. Subsequent counselling may be at the Penitent-form or in a quiet room. He will ensure that the seeker's name and address are registered.

(*e*) Another significant task is that of the literature evangelist. It is not just a question of disposing of *The War Cry* and other Army publications; it is a way of taking the gospel to those who will not otherwise be confronted with it. Wherever this can be done, in meetings, in the streets, from door to door, in market places, outside pleasure resorts, in hospitals, in restaurants and public houses and many other places, salvation soldiers should eagerly avail themselves of the opportunity to evangelize. Small musical parties could enliven such occasions and there should be a willingness to take time to use every opportunity to talk with individuals. Taking up even a small amount of literature evangelism is valuable and will provide an individual spiritual discipline which will bring blessing to the whole corps.

(*f*) Wherever possible, corps are undertaking practical service in the community. Local circumstances indicate on what lines such tasks of practical Christianity should be tackled. Here, as in the purely spiritual work of the corps, the aim and purpose must be to influence the people for Christ and for surrender to His claims.

(*g*) No soldier must imagine that he is not needed in the life and work of the corps. There is a task for everyone, and not being asked to take up a definite duty is no indication that he is not required. In such a situation the correct thing is to turn to the Commanding Officer and discuss the matter.

(*h*) Positions of responsibility and authority in the corps are filled by soldiers appointed as local officers without remuneration. Certain of these local officers together form the census board and as such are members of the corps council. They, with others who are appointed for a year at a time, advise and assist the Commanding Officer concerning the work of the corps council according to the regulations governing such work.

4. *The Young People's Corps:*

(*a*) The work among the children and young people is the responsibility of the young people's corps, but should be an object of the interest of the whole corps. The supreme purpose of the young people's work is to bring children and young people to Jesus Christ and to help them discover and use their talents as fighting soldiers in the ranks of The Salvation Army.

(*b*) The main work of the young people's corps consists of meetings suitable for the respective groups. On Sundays the chief points of the Christian faith are dealt with in the directory meeting, Bible instruction is given in the company meeting, and a young people's salvation meeting is held at least once weekly, either on Sundays or during the week. One Sunday each quarter is set apart to be a Decision Sunday, when young people who do not profess conversion are invited to seek the Saviour, though this does not preclude children from seeking

Him in other meetings. There are weekly club activities, a corps cadet class, junior soldiers' meeting, practices and spiritual meetings for musical sections, various preparatory classes, and other activities.

(*c*) The local officers of the young people's corps should possess love for and aptitude in dealing with children and young people.

(*d*) The young people's work will be judged successful in as much as it produces senior soldiers who are truly converted, well acquainted with the Scriptures, imbued with the principles of The Salvation Army and zealous fighters for God. Converted young people may, having attained the age of at least seven years, be enrolled as junior soldiers. Upon attaining the age of fourteen years a converted young person may sign the Articles of War and be accepted for senior soldiership.

CHAPTER XI
THE SALVATION SOLDIER

SECTION 1. A REPRESENTATIVE OF SALVATIONISM

1. No one is a full member of The Salvation Army who has not been enrolled and sworn-in as a soldier of a corps. The preparatory stage of recruit or junior soldier is a period of learning what is involved in soldiership and of proving oneself worthy of acceptance to full membership of the Army. A person having been converted must first be accepted as a recruit and attend preparatory classes before becoming eligible for soldiership. A junior soldier after attaining the age of fourteen years, and after having signed the Articles of War may be transferred to the senior corps.

2. The senior census board is empowered to accept new soldiers and must satisfy itself that the recruits and junior soldiers concerned are truly converted, that they have read *Orders and Regulations for Soldiers* and undertake to fulfil the duties of soldiership as set forth therein, and that they have read and signed the Articles of War and are prepared, before their enrolment, to affirm their adherence to the rules and promises expressed in that document.

3. Having been duly sworn-in under the flag and become a soldier of The Salvation Army, the comrade concerned will understand that people will regard him as a representative of the Movement, whose uniform he is expected to wear when on duty, but whose principles he is pledged to abide by at all times, also in surroundings where no one is aware of his identity. Conduct of which the soldier would not approve in uniform must not be indulged in at other times. Courtesy, kindness and helpfulness which the uniform would seem to demand must not be neglected even if he is wearing private clothes.

4. It is quite common for people to form their opinion of large groups of people on the basis of isolated experience. Such generalization may be unfair and undeserved, but the phenomenon works both ways. Let the soldier remember that he, as a representative of Salvationism, may help to confirm the worthy image which the Movement has in many parts of the world and among all kinds of people, though on the other hand he may create active dislike of the whole Army by unworthy or discourteous conduct.

5. As a Salvation Army soldier he will need to be as well informed about the Movement as possible. He should therefore study its publications, especially *The War Cry*, for up-to-date information as well as for his own edification. Other Army literature will enrich his

own inner life and will make him increasingly helpful to the non-Salvationist who is interested in the Movement.

6. One feature of Salvationism about which the soldier should be thoroughly informed is the practice of uniform-wearing. It was introduced as a natural consequence of the Movement adopting military lines and the name of an Army, and has proved itself productive of numerous advantages. For example:

(a) it singles out its wearer as a professing Christian;

(b) it is an invitation to the people to avail themselves of the help in spiritual and social matters which a Salvationist may be expected to render;

(c) it helps its wearer to remember to walk worthy of his calling;

(d) it is a protection in surroundings where he might otherwise be molested;

(e) it creates an immediate feeling of comradeship with any other wearers of the uniform;

(f) it opens the way for the soldier to act as the representative of the Army whatever his errand may be. This consideration makes it imperative to keep the uniform neat and clean, and to ensure that it follows the regulation lines authorized for the territory or command concerned.

7. The uniform of The Salvation Army is not intended to isolate its wearer from other people, but is rather, as already mentioned, the dress of ' a servant of all '. It does not imply a rebuke to sinners, but rather a loving greeting from the Heavenly Father. It is no claim to superiority and no attempt to proclaim Salvationism as a condition of salvation, but is a testimony about the grace of God in Christ.

SECTION 2. SAVED TO SAVE

1. Just as the central word of the name of his Movement is salvation, so the salvation soldier will recollect that his Articles of War begin with a declaration about having personally received it and conclude with a dedication to personal work for the salvation of the whole world. In other words, the soldier knows that he is saved—to save! The love of Christ requires him to make an unreserved commitment to His service.

2. Behind this unreserved dedication to the salvation war is the assurance ' that the sure and only way to remedy all the evils in the world is by bringing men to submit themselves to the government of the Lord Jesus Christ ' (Articles of War).

3. The salvation soldier must not therefore comfort himself with the knowledge that he is taking part in the collective endeavours of an association of people. He is also an individual agent of the Lord Jesus and has to show personal enterprise in the endeavours to win people one by one. He will be surprised how the numbers will grow if every soldier wins one person each year.

4. The salvation soldier must not be satisfied with a corps, however flourishing and attractive and strong, which is not above all striving to win new people for Christ. Soldiers who are truly saved must pray and work earnestly to save others.

5. While the soldier will be gripped by the assurance that ' all have need of God's salvation ', he will generally be well advised to give special attention to those with whom he has much in common and whose problems and situation in life resemble his own. An adolescent is likely to be the best ambassador of Christ to another young person, a housewife to another, a converted alcoholic to one who is seeking deliverance from the same chains,

and so forth. But the most important thing is to be led by the Holy Spirit and to act with tender love, assured that the motto, ' Every soldier a soul-winner ', is pleasing to God.

SECTION 3. WILLING WORKER AND GLAD GIVER

1. The salvation soldier will not forget the promise he gave when signing the Articles of War, to spend all the time, strength, money and influence he can in supporting and carrying on the salvation war. He will not regard his time as his own. His strength has also been given to him to be used on behalf of the Giver, God Himself. And his money is not his in the sense that he can use it as he himself pleases. The soldier is God's steward, and so he must be a willing worker and a glad giver.

2. ' It is required in stewards, that a man be found faithful ' (1 Corinthians 4: 2). The soldier must seek the guidance of God concerning the use of his time, so that he does not neglect his daily employment, the duties to his home and family, his continued training, his health, etc. In these matters also he must be a faithful steward. But as a soldier he will realize that the cause of the Kingdom of God must hold a high place among his priorities. His presence at meetings is of importance not only to himself, but will stimulate this part of the work and afford the soldier opportunities to make his own contribution to the programme. Visitation, literature evangelism, practical help in the homes of the sick, the poor, the over-worked, at the corps, etc., the duties and tasks entrusted to the soldier must all be taken into consideration as the steward of God plans the use of his time.

3. As stewards of God each soldier of a corps must feel individual responsibility for financing the work. Each

corps is expected to be self-supporting to the highest possible degree as well as raising money for the work in general. A trustworthy steward will endeavour to settle as conscientiously as possible how great a proportion of his income should be devoted to the Lord's work and how the Lord's money should be dispensed. The Bible and Christian tradition mention the paying of tithes. For practical purposes there may be various ways of calculating a person's real income, after taxes and other deductions, but the principle is clear. Not a few Salvationists give one-half of their tithes as their regular contribution to the corps (' cartridge money '), and from the other half they find contributions to the Self-Denial Appeal, collections and special purposes. One frequent result is that those who have become regular tithers after a while go beyond this amount and pay in addition a ' sacrifice ' for a special purpose. A sense of stewardship makes it easy to be a joyful giver.

4. Generous personal giving will make the soldier confident when undertaking the duty of soliciting funds for the Army, a duty which demands time and strength. However, as a steward of God the soldier will willingly give both, knowing that the Army's work is out of all proportion to its size. It is therefore not out of place to ask the public to help financially.

SECTION 4. PUBLIC SPEAKING

1. Because it has always been the conviction of The Salvation Army that those who have experienced the salvation of Christ are called to be witnesses for Him, right from the moment of his conversion the convert should be prepared to witness by his word of testimony. Such speaking in public has proved to be not only a means of encouraging God's people and of calling sinners,

but of confirming the speakers in their new-found experience.

2. It continues to be the intention of the Army to maintain such a ministry of personal testimony rather than to allow a one-man ministry to develop to the exclusion of the soldiers, old and young. At times, comrades who have acquired more ability to speak in public should also be given the responsibility to give addresses on texts or topics. It is essential for speakers to know what task they have been given. To give a sermon when they have been asked to relate a personal spiritual experience is as great a mistake as to limit themselves to personal observations when they are expected to expound the word of God.

3. Even if the soldier has not been given notice of it before the event, it is good for him to go to the meeting with some idea of what he should say, should it be thought suitable for him to speak. Naturally, if he has received notice beforehand, he will prepare his remarks by study, meditation and prayer.

4. The message, if truly given by the Spirit, will be living and practical. It must be expressed in simple words which are not beyond the understanding of the listeners. A well-chosen illustration will help to stimulate their attention. The address should not be too lengthy. It is better to conclude while the hearers regretfully feel that they would have liked to hear more, than to go on until they sigh with relief when the speaker at last has finished.

5. Whether giving his testimony or delivering an address, the speaker must keep clearly in mind what main result he is driving at and what part of his public he is particularly wishing to reach. General rambling will dissipate everybody's attention.

6. The more the speaker is himself gripped by the message, the more likely he is to captivate his hearers. He should beware of the temptation simply to make an impression rather than to glorify his Saviour.

7. A soldier must try to do the people good—to get them saved and blessed there and then. He must speak as the servant of God, considering the seriousness of the business and the uncertainty of ever having an opportunity to speak to the same people again. In short, he must speak as a dying man to dying men.

SECTION 5. LIFELONG COMMITMENT

1. No person will wish to be enrolled as a soldier unless he has come to the conclusion that ' The Salvation Army has been raised up by God and is sustained and directed by Him '. He will take time to acquaint himself thoroughly with the Movement before applying for soldiership on the conditions outlined in the Articles of War.

2. The junior soldier, preparing for transfer to the senior corps, will have studied the Articles of War. Especially in his case it will be necessary to emphasize the declaration contained in the last paragraph of the Articles that enrolment as a soldier is arranged as the result of his free-will decision. No one must be subject to undue pressure to become a salvation soldier. Parental wish, family traditions, the desire to join a musical section of the corps, etc., are not legitimate motives for becoming a soldier. The salvation soldier must volunteer for service, compelled only by the redemptive love of Christ.

3. No one must become a soldier as an experiment or with mental reservations as to the length of his ' service for the salvation of the whole world '. Only those who

are fully determined, by God's help, to be true soldiers of
The Salvation Army till they die can rightly take the holy
vows involved in the swearing-in ceremony.

4. Every Salvationist should realize that the dedication
of his life as a soldier is above all an act between himself
and God. At times he is likely to be disappointed in the
Army, since it is an association of human beings and
therefore imperfect. But his duty is to the ideal Army,
such as God wishes it to be, and he will find that if he
strives wholeheartedly to be faithful to this ideal, he will
have neither time nor mind to criticize the shortcomings
of others. His business will be to make sure that The
Salvation Army is better because of his life and work in it
than it would be without him. And without doubt he will
find that there are comrades who give him an inspiring and
encouraging example. He will thank God for men and
women in the Army who are filled with the Holy Spirit
and truly sanctified, and he will feel certain that God has
called him to spend his life in the fellowship of such
comrades.

5. One of the happy developments from the transfor-
mation of The Christian Mission to The Salvation Army
was the following of the military model for Christian warfare. A vital requirement for all armies is discipline
involving self-forgetfulness for the sake of common
success, and obedience to the commands of leaders making
combined action purposeful and effective. The joyful
acceptance of such hard campaigning has been blessed by
the Holy Spirit in the winning of converts in all parts of
the world. What is required of the salvation soldier is
not a blind unintelligent obedience, but a self-discipline
which enters into every aspect of life, and is in direct
contrast to the self-indulgent outlook of the world.

SECTION 6. THE CALL TO OFFICERSHIP

1. When enlisting in the Army, the soldier amongst other things solemnly promised to serve and obey God ' through time and in eternity '. He will understand that this pledge concerns every detail of his life, so that tasks that seem quite ordinary are done to the glory of God and in obedience to His will. But he will also realize that the salvation war requires the performance of special duties, to which God calls suitable persons by various means. No call can be more important than that to officership. It is a matter which must be decided irrespective of the likes or dislikes of the person concerned. It is God who calls, and He is able to make His will so plain that the one He singles out for the unique honour of being His messenger will not need to doubt it.

2. Young Salvationists, observing the importance to the Army of the service of its officers, can hardly avoid the question whether they themselves should become officers. It is a question which must not be left open until it is too late, nor must it be written off because the young person wishes to escape it. On the other hand he must not lightly offer for officership just because the thought appeals to him. The call comes from God to those it concerns. The most important thing is to be wholly dedicated to God and willing to listen to Him and to follow His will.

3. Obviously, in a matter of this description, communion with God is the most important necessity. The call, if it is genuine, is from Him. He sees the innermost thoughts of His young servants. He knows whether they are unwilling, whether they are busy finding excuses for rejecting the call, and whether they try to prove that the whole matter is a mistake. God knows also how far

enthusiasm in the opposite direction stems from right motives. In the light of God the soul sees its inmost motives. Utter honesty and sincerity before God and willingness to let Him have His way, will bring victory and peace.

4. The young soldier who is troubled about the question of the call will be unable to ignore the urgent need. God has given the Army endless possibilities to enlarge the Kingdom of God and to come to the aid of suffering mankind—' The harvest truly is great,' as Jesus said (Luke 10: 2), ' but the labourers are few.' He continued: ' pray ye therefore the Lord of the harvest, that He would send forth labourers into His harvest.' Persistent prayer for more officers will lead others who have the necessary qualifications to go out into His harvest. And it will also reveal whether this need is not also a call to the one interceding so earnestly.

5. Ever burdened with the urgency and immensity of the Army's calling in a sinning and suffering world, the Founder warned against the tendency to brush aside this sense of obligation. He wrote: ' " Not called", did you say? " Not heard the call ", I think you should say. He has been calling loudly ever since He spoke yours sins forgiven—if you are forgiven at all—entreating and beseeching you to be His ambassador.' To William Booth, the need was in a very real sense a call. He would argue that unless there is a special task which has a compelling hold on the mind of the young Salvationist, the overwhelming likelihood is that his life's work should be that of an officer. Let him look at his qualifications. Is he truly saved? Has he got sound mental powers? Is he well and free from bodily defects? Is his education of a standard which at least corresponds to the average around him? If his answer to these questions is in the affirmative, could it be

that his plea that he lacks God's call is in reality an indication that he does not want to accept it?

6. There have been young Salvationists who have felt that they were ill-equipped for the work of an officer. Indeed, there is a sense in which no officer can feel that he measures up to his high calling in every respect. But the experience of countless officers is that God honours the willingness of His people to serve Him in obedience to His call to the best of their ability. No young Salvationist must take upon himself the fateful responsibility of concluding that he is not suitable. Having sought the guidance of the Holy Spirit, he should submit his application for officership to his leaders and be prepared to accept their decision.

7. Irrespective of age, all salvation soldiers should pray earnestly for more labourers to harvest the Lord's crop, and especially for any in the corps in whom they see prospective officers. They must, however, beware of constantly reminding them, thus creating a contra-suggestion. Never must it happen that a young person, however useful to the work of his corps, is persuaded to abandon any thoughts of officership which he is entertaining.

SECTION 7. THE CARE OF THE BODY

The Christian view of the human body has its roots in the Old Testament, where man is seen as a unity of body and soul. Body and soul should not be contrasted with one another, as they were in ancient Greece and still are in many parts of the East.

The fact that Jesus shared to the full our common humanity means that the life of the body is itself sacred.

Therefore, the Salvationist will not despise or misuse his body. Seeing it can be the instrument of God's

purpose, he will endeavour—insofar as this is possible—
to keep it in a healthy, vigorous state.

Bodily health is a good thing. This means that the
Salvationist will seek the best medical advice when he is
unwell, and at all times ensure that he is properly
nourished by eating the right kind of food in proper
quantities. He will also be sensible in his choice of the
clothes he wears.

The Salvationist will be concerned about personal
hygiene, realizing that cleanliness is both healthy and a
reflection of the Christian standards he has embraced.

The Salvationist will seek to ensure that he gets
sufficient fresh air, exercise and sleep. This is Christian
common sense. For example, a person who has in-
sufficient sleep is likely to be both irritable and a poor
workman.

The basic Christian principle is that the body is the
temple of the Holy Spirit (1 Corinthians 6: 19; 2
Corinthians 6: 16) and therefore must not be defiled.

SECTION 8. THE IMPROVEMENT OF THE MIND

Jesus said that the ' first ', that is, the most important,
commandment was that man should love God with all his
heart and soul and mind and strength (Mark 12: 28–30).
The Salvationist will therefore seek to improve his mental
powers, so that his love of God and service for God will
be all the more effective.

In these days of universal education, of library services
and of cheap paperback books there is no longer any
excuse for ignorance.

It is easy to fall into slovenly mental habits and the
Salvationist will be on his guard. The mind, like the body,
needs daily exercise.

The habit of reading should be part of every Salvationist's life. That he will read the Bible should go with-

out saying, but he will also read other literature in order to make his service effective.

The Christian gospel must be related to the present day. The Salvationist will therefore need to encourage an awareness of the contemporary situation and its needs. He will seek to educate himself concerning the Army, the wider Church, the lives of good men, Christian theology. If he does not know where to begin, he will ask advice from those who can give the necessary guidance—older soldiers and officers.

A great deal of current literature and journalism is of little help to the Christian. The Salvationist will acquaint himself with this only insofar as it will equip him for his Christian witness.

Being interested in what is happening in and to the world—for it is God's world—the Salvationist should read at least one serious newspaper, and will watch news and documentary television programmes as occasion demands.

The habit of observation should be cultivated. Each day should add to the Salvationist's knowledge of life and his understanding of the gospel. Wisdom is more than knowledge. Wisdom is the right use of knowledge.

SECTION 9. THE USE OF LEISURE

Leisure is a necessity rather than a luxury. In all life there is the alternative between night and day, sleeping and waking, play and work. The true function of leisure is to recreate. The word ' recreation ' indicates the way in which leisure should be used. That which recreates a man's power of body, mind or spirit is both legitimate and desirable.

The Salvationist will not engage in any pastime that is morally wrong. For example, cruel spectacles and lewd shows which are detrimental to the well-being of partici-pants or spectators must stand condemned.

It is recognized that because television and radio bring all kinds of entertainments into the home itself, the Salvationist must learn self-discipline. It is necessary for him to discriminate between the helpful and the unhelpful programme.

Time spent in personal recreation should be related to the claims of God's work. In the Salvationist's life, worship and service each have a claim that must be given priority.

The Salvationist should also consider the legitimate demands of home life. No selfish indulgence should take priority.

Interest in such excellent things as, for example, music and sport can become excessive. It is the wisely disciplined person who derives most from life. The Salvationist will use his leisure to keep himself informed and to extend the range of his usefulness by developing his aptitudes and capacities. He is responsible for the use of his own potentiality.

The Salvationist will be concerned lest his personal example should be harmed by his leisure pursuits. With this in mind, he will ' abstain from all appearance of evil ' (1 Thessalonians 5: 22). He will seek to ensure that his conduct does not increase the pressure of temptation upon others.

In keeping himself informed of the kind of world in which the gospel must be preached, the Salvationist will be confronted with much that is sordid. He will, however, fill his mind with ' whatsoever things are true, whatsoever things are honest, whatsoever things are just, whatsoever things are pure, whatsoever things are lovely, whatsoever things are of good report ' (Philippians 4: 8).

In connection with the use of leisure, it is not possible to be specific for every individual, in all situations. A basic principle that can always be applied, however, is this: leisure time spent in personal recreation should be related to:

(*a*) The claims of God's work.

(*b*) The demands of home life.

(*c*) The requirements of health.

The New Testament warns believers against loving ' the world ' (1 John 2: 15–17). It tells them not to be ' conformed ' to this world (Romans 12: 2). Christians are to be ' in ' the world, but not ' of ' the world.

This teaching the Salvationist desires to take seriously. It means that the direction he wishes his life to take, and the standards by which he desires to live, are determined by God's revelation in Jesus Christ. Our Lord did not sever Himself from men, but He refused to let their self-centredness determine His pattern of life. He loved the world, but fought against ' the spirit of the world '. The Salvationist will seek to do the same.

SECTION 10. TIMES OF SICKNESS

Few people escape sickness altogether. The Salvationist's faith should enable him to face sickness in a positive way. He will, of course, accept the necessary medical help and co-operate wisely with the doctor or hospital authorities. He will also ask for the blessing of God, seeking to discover the divine will.

Jesus was on the side of health. He regarded disease as part of the kingdom of evil (Luke 13: 16). This must mean that God's ideal will for all men is health of body, mind and spirit.

The Salvationist will not, therefore, blame God for his sickness, but will accept his lot in the realization that he is bearing part of the burden of mankind. Many saints have had to bear physical weakness and sickness over long periods. The Salvationist will seek to endure without complaining.

It is proper to make provision for one's own death (that is, by the making of a will, etc.) while in good health. Times of sickness, however, underline the fact of mortality. For the believer the end of earthly life need have no fears. In life or in death, he is in the safe hands of God.

When others in the family are sick, the Salvationist should be sympathetic, patient and practical. This also applies to the sickness of neighbours, workmates and friends.

Christians should be sensitive to other people's needs. No Salvationist should exploit the need and weakness of others but, by being available at such times, he may have the opportunity of speaking the right word and of witnessing for Christ.

CHAPTER XII

THE ARMY SPIRIT

SECTION 1. A SIGNIFICANT EXPRESSION

1. From the early days of The Salvation Army 'the Army spirit' has been a characteristic expression in the vocabulary of the Movement. It has been a way of indicating that certain qualities, convictions and principles have always been accepted as desirable and necessary. Moreover, whatever success has attended the work of the Movement must, under God, to a large extent be explained by the soldiers having been animated and possessed by them.

2. Important as it is to be acquainted with the Army's rules and regulations, it is still more important to understand and be possessed by the Army spirit. This concluding chapter attempts an analysis of the significance of the expression without claiming to penetrate the

whole subject. The Holy Spirit of God will reveal to true Salvationists how they can exhibit that practical, loving and self-denying attitude to the straying, sinning and suffering world for which Christ died, which is the hallmark of the genuine Army spirit.

SECTION 2. STRONG FAITH

1. The salvation soldier believes in the God and Father of the Lord Jesus Christ. Christ trusted in His heavenly Father with a childlike and perfect confidence, and the soldier wishes to be like his Lord in this as in other respects. There is not one thing about which a child of God may not talk to his Heavenly Father.

2. The salvation soldier accepts the assurance of Jesus about answer to prayer offered in His name and concerning His Kingdom.

3. The soldier knows that Christ is a mighty Saviour. He therefore has strong faith for the salvation of sinners for whom there is, humanly speaking, little hope.

4. The history of The Salvation Army abounds in examples of strong faith in God through which men and women exhibiting the Army spirit have secured victories over evil, obtained help in distress and witnessed numerous miracles. In fact, the Army is itself a monument to the efficacy of faith.

SECTION 3. INFECTIOUS JOY

1. The salvation soldier is not only aware of and acquainted with the terrible ravages of evil in the life of men and women but he has himself experienced the saving and keeping power of the Lord Jesus Christ. He has moreover witnessed the transforming power of the Saviour in the lives of the worst kind of sinners. He cannot but be filled with joy over the triumphs of grace.

| Chap. XII | The Army Spirit | Sect. 4 |

2. The daily proofs he has of the goodness of God and the power of His might make him ' rejoice with exceeding great joy '.

3. The salvation soldier is a happy Christian because he has numerous opportunities of serving his fellow men, winning sinners for Christ and testifying about His Lord.

4. Salvationists are sure that they will glorify their Lord by living as rejoicing Christians. The world has gloom and sadness enough of its own. The joy of the Lord is the strength of the Army spirit.

SECTION 4. BURNING COMPASSION

1. William Booth said more than once that the Army was the religious organization of the friendless. Scholars remark upon the Army's combination of evangelical zeal for and practical care of the unwanted and outcasts of society. The Army's compassion for the underprivileged is seen by these writers as exceptional among religious bodies of a similar type.

2. This compassion is seen in steady regular service to the needy. Typical is the absence of proselytizing, i.e. of the desire to secure adherents through social relief work. On the other hand the Army has shown vivid awareness of the fact that human beings cannot be permanently helped unless their personality problems are reached. The spiritual salvation of the underdog has throughout the years been the deepest concern of Salvationists.

3. The Army spirit requires continued sensitivity to the plight of the down-and-outs, the forgotten, the dregs of society. Rightly or wrongly the Movement has been called an example of ' the churches of the dispossessed, who through their religious discipline rise socially—and forget " the new poor " '. The Salvation Army must not

88

become so much of a middle class Movement that it forgets ' the rock whence it is hewn '. It is called to proclaim salvation to all classes, but its special glory should be its concern for and its ability to appeal to the lowest and most forgotten, and to be their champions in every respect. It belongs to the Army spirit to remember those whom others forget.

Section 5. Going for Souls and Going for the Worst

1. ' Souls ' is an expression which must not be mis-understood. The salvation soldier must always remember to pay attention to the whole man. The basic conviction of Salvationism is that man's specific need as a human being, which makes him different from all other created beings, is his need of fellowship with God. Man has not been helped as he needs to be helped if he has been provided with food, clothes and shelter, to the neglect of his problems of personality and his moral and spiritual difficulties.

2. It belongs to the Army spirit to abstain from such display of superiority as is calculated to make ' the worst ' feel uncomfortable and out of place. Salvationists must not be snobs. The Army should be truly both *of* the people and *for* the people.

Section 6. The Army of the Helping Hand

1. This epithet is often used as a public relations phrase but not without justification. Spectacular ' action ' in a given situation or an emergency is usually instigated and directed by leaders of the Army, willingly and efficiently supported by a host of workers. Such ' action ' is certainly evidence of the Army spirit.

2. But the Army spirit is also expressed in the spontaneous action of the individual soldier. Daily life brings with it situations in which a ' good turn ' can mean vital aid to someone when he most requires it. A readiness to help is the motive behind the ' Helping Hand ': the salvation soldier whose motto is ' With heart to God and hand to man ' is saved to serve as well as to save.

3. It must never happen that a genuine appeal for help of any kind is made to a Salvationist without meeting sympathetic attention. Even when the soldier cannot be of actual service, he must show concern and kindness. The Army spirit demands it.

SECTION 7. SOLDIERS BOUND FOR GLORY

1. The Army spirit has always shown itself through the joyful way in which salvation soldiers have contemplated their ' march to Zion '. Life is not a weary journey. Despite dangers and trials, the soldier preserves the assurance that he is bound for Glory.

2. The end of the journey is not therefore contemplated as something dark and sombre. The faithful soldier does not die. He is promoted to Glory. Much as his dear ones and his comrades will miss him, they do not mourn as those without hope but give thanks to God for his life and work. Their tears are the natural expression of their sense of loss but they are mingled with gratitude for all God has given them through the one He has now called to his reward.

3. The funeral arrangements must not therefore through any detail express the hopelessness of those who do not know the risen and living Christ. Instead of black the Army's funeral colour is white, and the flags which wave at the graveside are draped with white ribbons. Soldiers will attend the funeral in uniform and can, if

they are so disposed, have a white ribbon round the sleeve of their tunic. The Army has ever regarded it as unsuitable for Salvationists to dress in mourning for a period after the funeral. Flowers are not forbidden at Army funerals, but it is definitely against Army principles to allow wastefulness in this as in any other connection.

4. Just as the life of the promoted comrade has aimed at the honour and glory of the Saviour, so the theme at his funeral should be praise for God's grace in Christ. The memorial meeting should avoid exaggerated tribute to human qualities, the aim being to encourage God's people to dedicate themselves afresh to the salvation war and to help the unconverted to seek the Lord.